A GUIDE TO PLANNING

coaching programmes

D0488299

ISBN 1 902523 00 8

Authors: Bill Galvin and Paul Ledger
Editor: Bill Galvin
Sub-editors: Penny Crisfield, Phil Larder and Clare Palmer
Typesetter: Lisa Furness

Cover photo courtesy of actionplus sports images
All other photos courtesy of **sports coach UK** and actionplus sports images

sports coach UK would like to thank Alan Lynn and Hamish Telfer for reviewing the resource.

Published on behalf of
sports coach UK by

sports coach UK
114 Cardigan Road
Headingley
Leeds LS6 3BJ
Tel: 0113-274 4802 Fax: 0113-275 5019
E-mail: coaching@sportscoachuk.org
Website: www.sportscoachuk.org

Patron: HRH The Princess Royal

Coachwise Solutions
Coachwise Ltd
Chelsea Close
Off Amberley Road
Armley
Leeds LS12 4HP
Tel: 0113-231 1310 Fax: 0113-231 9606
E-mail: enquiries@coachwisesolutions.co.uk
Website: www.coachwisesolutions.co.uk

Preface

Coaching is about improving performance. Rather than hope that this improvement might just happen, coaches at all levels plan programmes of preparation to ensure they, their performers and their teams achieve their goals.

Many different factors contribute to sports performance. These include lifestyle factors such as careers, education, work, finances and health as well as the performer's physical, technical and psychological preparation. Tactics and teamwork may also be important issues, depending on your sport. Systematic planning is the only way to ensure that coach and performer can manage all these factors efficiently and effectively.

This pack is for coaches who wish to improve their ability to plan programmes for their performers over a season, year or longer period. In it, you will learn about the principles of planning and the theoretical foundations of coaching programmes, such as periodization. The activities will help you to apply your new skills and knowledge to your own sport. Once you have worked through the pack, you should be able to:

- generate information on your sport, performers and/or team to assist your planning
- integrate all components of performance into individual and team training programmes
- explain and apply the adaptation process
- periodize the year into training phases of different emphasis
- design balanced training programmes to meet the lifestyle needs of your performers
- adjust the seasonal plan when unexpected events occur
- identify appropriate ways to assess and monitor performance
- identify areas where you may require further information or personal development.

Key to symbols used in the text

 An activity.

 Approximate length of time to be spent on the activity.

? Stop and consider.

Throughout this pack, the pronouns he, she, him, her and so on are interchangeable and intended to be inclusive of both males and females. It is important in sport, as elsewhere, that both genders have equal status and opportunities.

Contents

Chapter One:	**Introduction to Planning**	Page
	1.0 What's in It for You?	1
	1.1 What is Planning?	1
	1.2 Planning and the Coaching Process	3
	1.3 Why Plan?	3
	1.4 Reflect on Your Current Planning Practice	8
	1.5 Recap and What Next?	10
Chapter Two:	**Gathering Information**	
	2.0 What's in It for You?	11
	2.1 The Components of Top Performance	11
	2.2 Analysis of a Performance Component	15
	2.3 Assessment of Your Performer/Team	18
	2.4 Analysing and Interpreting Results	25
	2.5 Recap and What Next?	27
Chapter Three:	**Profiling Needs and Action Planning**	
	3.0 What's in It for You?	29
	3.1 Performance Profiling	29
	3.2 Team Profiling	33
	3.3 Setting Goals	35
	3.4 Types of Goals	38
	3.5 Recap and What Next?	41
Chapter Four:	**Adaptation and Training Principles**	
	4.0 What's in It for You?	43
	4.1 Principles of Training	43
	4.2 The Process of Adaptation	48
	4.3 Recap and What Next?	54
Chapter Five:	**Periodization**	
	5.0 What's in It for You?	55
	5.1 Training Periodization	56
	5.2 Planning Macro Cycles	56
	5.3 Meso Cycle Planning	64
	5.4 Micro Cycle Planning	71
	5.5 The Annual Plan	76
	5.6 Long-term Performer Development Programmes	79
	5.7 Recap and What Next?	79

Chapter Six: **Time and Lifestyle Management**

    6.0   What's in It for You?   81

    6.1   Maximising Training Time   82

    6.2   Lifestyle Management   87

    6.3   Overcoming Unexpected Events   92

    6.4   Recap and What Next?   95

Chapter Seven: **Monitoring Progress**

    7.0   What's in It for You?   97

    7.1   Performance Indicators   98

    7.2   Recording the Data   103

    7.3   Performers' Logbooks   106

    7.4   Recap and What Next?   116

Appendix A: **Useful Planning and Monitoring Tools**   119

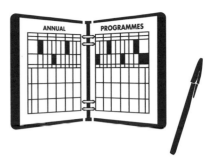

CHAPTER ONE
Introduction to Planning

1.0 What's in It for You?

This chapter provides an introduction to planning, explains what it entails and why it is important for all sports coaches. On completion of this chapter, you should be able to:

- describe the planning process
- explain the importance of planning to performance in your sport
- assess your own knowledge and abilities in the field of planning.

1.1 What is Planning?

Consider the following quote about preparation for performance from Jurgen Gröbler, coach to the gold medal winners in the coxless pairs at the Atlanta Olympics, Redgrave and Pinsent.

> *Know what to expect, prepare for it as much as possible and don't lose focus.*

Having accurate and relevant information on which to base your training programmes is central to this philosophy. Being clear about what *you want to achieve* is vital, but you must also know precisely *what you have to do* to achieve it. This means knowing your sport, your own performer or team and the opposition very, very well. Planning programmes of preparation is a systematic process which requires you to answer three questions:

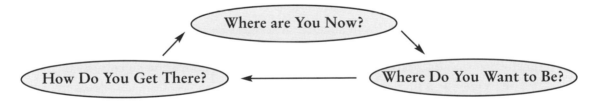

Figure 1: The planning process

Where Are You Now?

You must have a clear and realistic picture of the current state of preparation of your performer or team. You must also know how that corresponds to the demands of your sport and the standard of opposition at the appropriate level of competition. A swimming coach preparing a performer for the Olympic Games will be aware of his performer's current and best times for the event. He will also know what he thinks the performer is capable of and have an idea of the times that are likely to win medals at the Games. However, really knowing your performers means more than knowing the results they are likely to produce. It means knowing their strengths and weaknesses in all the components that make up the performance.

There are important planning tools which may be used at this stage of the process. Techniques for performer assessment and performance profiling will probably be familiar to you. In Chapters Two and Three you will use them to help plan your overall programme. If you feel you need further help in these areas, you will be referred to other sources where the topics are covered in more detail.

Where Do You Want to Be?

It is important to clarify the performer or team's *dream goal,* as it will shape the entire planning process, provide a focus for his or her commitment, and ensure a common purpose for coach, performer and/or team. This goal may seem unattainable unless it is broken into smaller, more achievable steps. The goal-setting process provides a framework for your training programmes. Chapter Three will help to sharpen your goal-setting skills.

How Do You Get There?

Having identified the gap between the performer's/team's aspirations and their current abilities, your task is to design and implement a programme that will take them from **where they are now** to **where they want to be.** All the components that contribute to successful performance must be included. The time-frames for the different phases of preparation must be determined and the contents of each phase should be clearly outlined.

A knowledge of planning principles is necessary if your planning is to be successful. This pack will develop your knowledge of the process of adaptation and the principles of periodization. You will then be able to divide your programme into separate phases which build into a complete and effective plan. Chapters Four and Five will assist you with this process.

Monitoring and Evaluation

A planning process is of limited value if it cannot be monitored and evaluated. Monitoring is the process of gathering information that will inform coach and performer about progress (or lack of it) towards the performer's goals. Evaluation involves making a judgement on the programme of preparation, and deciding whether or not to amend the plans. Chapter Seven will help you decide how you will monitor and evaluate your programme.

1.2 Planning and the Coaching Process

It should now be clear that planning is central to the role of the coach as it provides a framework for the entire process of preparation for performance. In *Planning Coaching Sessions,*[1] the following model of coaching was introduced:

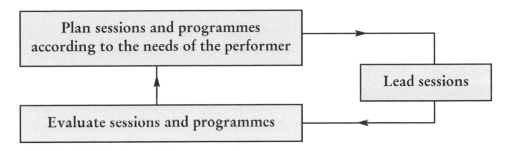

Figure 2: The coaching process

Formal planning does not mean that your programmes are rigid and inflexible. There are many factors affecting preparation programmes that cannot be predicted, such as personal events, weather, or reactions of the performer mentally and physically to a given training load. For that reason, longer term programmes must be flexible as the performer and coach may need to adapt the programme in response to unpredictable events. Chapter Six will help you to design a balanced programme of preparation that takes a holistic approach to performer development.

1.3 Why Plan?

For performers, achieving goals means performing at the peak of their ability. To reach this peak, all components of performance must be at an optimal level. It is the coach's task to ensure that the performer's programme of preparation includes all these components, and that the performer can peak in all of them simultaneously.

Performance components are not developed in isolation but build on each other and are supported by other performance components. Power, for example, may only be developed when the appropriate levels of strength have been achieved, and power training may be enhanced by previous training in areas such as flexibility. All training effects are cumulative – blocks that build on previously laid blocks. These building blocks make complex structures and a coach requires sound planning skills to ensure the structures are well founded.

In some sports, coaches and performers must make decisions about their priorities among different components – rugby players cannot devote all their time and effort to becoming stronger, at the expense of their endurance. Similarly the multi-event performer cannot afford to improve at one event but deteriorate in the others. Only detailed planning can ensure the right decisions are made on training content and balance.

---

1   Available from **Coachwise 1st4sport** (tel 0113-201 5555 or visit www.1st4sport.com).

Team Games

In team games, planning occurs at two levels. Individuals will follow their own training programmes to meet positional and individual needs, and the team will have a programme of preparation which aims to produce an efficient and competitive unit through a synthesis of the individuals within it. These programmes will overlap and complement each other to a greater or lesser extent depending on the time of season. In the off-season, individuals will follow their own individual programmes almost exclusively. During the competitive phase, the team will train as a unit at every available opportunity. The performance of the team as a unit is dependent on the performance of the individuals within it. The challenge for the coach is to balance the needs of the individual with the needs of the team. Detailed planning is the key.

The following activity will help you to clarify the advantages of planning in your situation, and assist you in avoiding the pitfalls that some planners discover as they work through the process.

ACTIVITY 1

1   Read the following pen pictures.

Pen Picture 1

Jake is a swimming coach who plans every session and every training cycle thoroughly. He sits down with each swimmer, his or her family, psychologist and any other relevant parties to plan the programme at yearly and four yearly intervals. In this way he attempts to take account of every variable that might affect performance. Every month he has a review and evaluation session with each swimmer. At this session, they will set goals for the following month and plan the monthly programme. Weekly planning sessions set the goals and content for each micro-cycle. After every training session, he reflects on the session with the swimmer and assesses whether goals set have been achieved. He then sets goals for the following session. The training programme evolves through the year and all goals are set as incremental improvements on the previous ones, in line with an overall target. Goals are mostly achieved. If it appears that a goal will not be achieved, the reason for it is thoroughly analysed and an adjusted goal set.

Pen Picture 2

Pete is an experienced rugby coach. He will decide on the content for each session with the players when they arrive at the ground. The performance of the team in the previous weekend's match will determine the content of the session. They will work on the aspects of performance that were not up to standard. Pete also believes that players must be enthusiastic about their training. If they want to train at a particular component, Pete will usually let them. He believes it is most important that players have an input into and enjoy the sessions. In the run-up to important matches, however, Pete will be more prescriptive with the players, ensuring that their training is at competition intensity. He will also take more interest in their lifestyle, as he believes that sufficient recovery and mental preparation are crucial in this phase.

Pen Picture 3

Geeta is a triathlon coach. She is very experienced and knows exactly what it takes to achieve success. She will be able to outline the precise session that her athletes will undergo in one month, or even six months from today. Planning is the key to her success as a coach. Long-term, intermediate and short-term goals are planned for each macro, meso and micro cycle from the beginning of the year. If athletes are not meeting their goals, she will push them harder to complete the required training. If they do not meet the required standards, they are better to stay out of her way. Discipline and hard work are the two key qualities required for success in the triathlon. The performance standards are set by the opposition, so the standards for performance at a certain level are not open for negotiation.

2 Based on the pen pictures and your own experience, list some advantages of using some kind of formal planning process to direct your preparation for competition:

-

-

-

-

3 Describe the pitfalls that are most obvious from poor planning:

-

-

-

-

4   What steps could be taken to avoid these pitfalls?

-

-

-

-

Now turn over.

1   Planning the performer's/team's programme will ensure that the coach:

- *includes all the factors contributing to performance in the preparation of the performer or team*
- *prioritises the performance components on the basis of the performer/team's strengths and weaknesses, and the time of season*
- *balances the time spent on the different performance components*
- *ensures that the training on different performance components is complementary*
- *can build appropriately on previous gains*
- *has the opportunity and the criteria with which to review and evaluate the programme and measure progress of his or her performers/team*
- *is able to use the planning process as a motivational tool with performer*
- *is able to determine his/her own coaching effectiveness.*

Thorough planning can help create confidence in performers, if they know that their preparation has been as complete as possible. Careful planning should result in a familiar and practised preparation for competition. This can minimise the pre-event anxiety that may cause problems for some performers.

2   If not managed properly, planning can:

- *be a very time-consuming process*
- *result in an inflexible approach, taking no account of individual differences*
- *result in performers not attaining over-ambitious goals and this may have a detrimental effect on confidence and motivation.*

3   These pitfalls may be avoided by :

- *adopting an incremental approach to planning (ie planning ahead in step-by-step phases) but within the framework of a master plan*
- *being flexible with the implementation of the plan*
- *integrating planning with the complete programme, rather than identifying particular times of the year as planning occasions.*

1.4 Reflect on Your Current Planning Practice

Consider the following quote, again from Jurgen Gröbler, referring to the Atlanta Olympics[1]:

> *The standard and quality of competition was exactly as I had expected and my training schedules had been geared to the performance standards that I predicted would win medals. As a coach, you must know exactly what is going on in your sport in order to stay on top. Training in the Olympic year always requires the highest volume of training, although this must be monitored carefully. Regular physiological assessments and performance tests allow you to modify training loads as appropriate, as well as providing a consistent measure of improvement.*

1   Coaching Focus No 34, Spring 1997: *Lessons from the Games.* Leeds, National Coaching Foundation. Available from **Coachwise 1st4sport** (tel 0113-201 5555 or visit www.1st4sport.com) while stocks last.

This may help you place the planning process in a practical context. Now you should consider how you use planning in your coaching at present. The following exercise will help you.

ACTIVITY 2

Give some thought to the following questions. Try to answer them honestly. Rate your ability from one to four, where one implies poor knowledge or ability in the area and four implies competence and confidence in the area.

(i) Can you outline the requirements for success in your sport, at the level of your performer or team?

  1   2   3   4

(ii) Are you able to profile your performers/team objectively against these requirements?

  1   2   3   4

(iii) How well do you understand the process of developing each requirement of your sport?

  1   2   3   4

(iv) Do you divide the training year into phases which allow for concentration on different components of performance?

  1   2   3   4

(v) Do you know why and how to manipulate the training load in the various training cycles?

  1   2   3   4

(vi) Are you satisfied that your performers peak at the right time and for the right occasions?

  1   2   3   4

(vii) Can you explain the physiological and psychological bases for peaking?

  1   2   3   4

(viii) Are you satisfied that you use assessment at the right times and for the right reasons?

  1   2   3   4

(ix) Do you use your plans as a tool to reflect upon your own practice?

  1   2   3   4

Now review your answers to the previous activity. Identify the aspects of planning programmes in which you feel less confident. (You will have scored yourself at one or two in these areas):

-
-
-

Ask yourself why you do not feel confident in these areas. Is it a lack of knowledge that inhibits you, or have you been unable to apply your knowledge to your present needs? Maybe you simply have not had time to think the problems through? Jot down the reasons for your lack of confidence in each of the areas you listed above.

In the space below, outline some goals that you will have achieved by the end of this pack. These goals should be related to the areas identified above as your weaker areas.

-
-
-
-

These goals should provide you with a framework for your study of this pack. However, you may find that you benefit equally from those chapters which provide a refresher course in the areas where you believe you are strong.

1.5 Recap and What Next?

This chapter has explained what planning is, outlined the reasons for planning and explained that the planning process is an integral part of coaching. You should now have an overview of the planning process and should be beginning to think about how you use planning in your coaching at present. This reflection is central to your use of this pack. It will help to make the content immediate and relevant, so that the pack will have a direct influence on your coaching.

In the following chapters, you will deconstruct the planning process; then you will examine each constituent part to find the format and procedures that best suit your sport and coaching style.

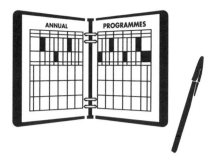

CHAPTER TWO
Gathering Information

2.0 What's in It for You?

Most sports are complex activities, which require performers to coordinate mental, physical, tactical and technical components in order to achieve their goals. These components are required to different degrees by different performers and at different levels of competition. It is vital that as coach, you have a clear picture of the demands of the sport for the level at which your team or performer will compete. This chapter will help you to identify these demands.

Once you have identified the demands of your sport, you will want to assess your performers in each of them. The information that you gather from these assessments will help you to ensure your coaching is effective and focused. By the end of this chapter, you should be able to:

• identify the components of top performance in your sport

• describe and analyse these components

• determine the optimal method of assessment for each of these components.

2.1 The Components of Top Performance

The starting point in developing any coaching programme should be to determine the overall demand that the sport places on the performer or team. It is usual to describe these demands as components of performance, under the following headings:

• physical (eg flexibility, speed)

• technical (eg backhand, shooting)

• tactical (eg anticipation, knowledge of opponents, match plan, decision making)

• mental (including mental skills and attitudes such as concentration and commitment).

Order of Importance

To establish the demands of your sport, you must identify the relative importance of each of these areas. Different sports will have different emphases. For example, a marathon runner's coach would probably rate them in the following order of importance:

1 Physical   2 Mental   3 Tactical   4 Technical.

The coach of a club rugby team, on the other hand, might say his or her order of priority was:

1 Technical   2 Tactical   3 Physical   4 Mental.

You might get different answers from different coaches within the same sport, reflecting their own perceptions of the importance of each area. Often you will find a different rating given for a novice performer compared with a more experienced performer. Try Activity Three.

ACTIVITY 3

1   Rate the importance of each area of performance for your performer/team from
1 (unimportant) to 5 (very important):

	Unimportant				Very important
Physical	1	2	3	4	5
Technical	1	2	3	4	5
Tactical	1	2	3	4	5
Mental	1	2	3	4	5

2   Now prioritise these areas, placing the most important against the number one and
the least important against number four.

1

2

3

4

3   List the areas in the order of importance in your sport for a:

novice performer/team   international performer/team

1   1

2   2

3   3

4   4

4   Briefly explain why the two lists are the same or why they differ:

*There is no correct answer – you may have highlighted the importance of one single area
or you may perceive several areas as being of equal importance. Your perception of the
relative importance of these areas will determine the way you plan your coaching
programme and allocate time.*

ACTIVITY 4

Imagine your performer or team producing a perfect performance or reflect on past outstanding performances in your sport. List those components that make up these top performances using the headings physical, technical, mental and tactical. Try to generate as many as you can.

Physical	Technical	Mental	Tactical

Now turn over.

You have probably listed a range of components for each factor. This demonstrates the variety of ingredients which contribute to a top performance – there are no right or wrong answers. This information forms the basis of your annual plan and will be used in many of the activities in the pack. You have probably identified some of the following components:

Mental Components

- *motivation*
- *relaxation*
- *control*
- *concentration*
- *confidence*
- *commitment.*

Physical Components

- *endurance*
- *speed*
- *power*
- *flexibility*
- *strength.*

Technical Components (for example)

- *match winning shooters (netball)*
- *backstroke – arm action (swimming)*
- *return of serve (tennis)*
- *length of stride (running).*

Tactical Components (for example)

- *setting target time (swimming)*
- *energy conservation (swimming)*
- *assessment of opposition strengths and weaknesses (netball)*
- *understanding of game/match plan (netball).*

Remember, in designing a training programme you will need to include the right quantity of each of these components – too much of one or too little of another can lead to a problem. The relative importance of these performance components will vary according to the time of the year, the level at which the performer/team competes and the goals the performer/team have set for the season or year (covered in more detail in Chapter Three).

If you are involved in a multi-sport (eg triathlon), you will have to consider the requirements of each event. If you are coaching a team game, you will need to examine each position and identify its specific demands, then plan your programmes accordingly. The individual requirements of a front row forward in rugby are, for example, very different from those of a scrum half or full back. The demands on the goalkeeper in hockey are different from those on the forwards.

If your sport has a strong tactical emphasis, you will highlight particular components of performance when you coach, in accordance with your game plan. A football coach, for example, will select particular skills and physical attributes as important, depending on his vision of the ideal game plan for the team. Different football coaches could have very different perspectives on the important technical and tactical or even physical and mental components depending on whether the game plan they sought to impose was based on possession or pressure. This is also true of other tactical sports.

2.2 Analysis of a Performance Component

In the last activity you were asked to break down top performance into components. In order to evaluate and develop performance in many of these components, it will be necessary to analyse it further. For example, a gymnastics coach might wish to identify separate sub-components in the component *flexibility*, in order to assess her performers more accurately, and plan a more detailed programme.

Flexibility – Sub-components

Hip abduction	Hip flexion	Hip extension
Shoulder abduction	Shoulder flexion	Shoulder extension
Spine abduction	Spine flexion	Spine extension

ACTIVITY 5

In Activity Four, you listed a range of components which make up a top performance in your sport. This activity asks you to analyse each component to determine the key sub-components. Examples from netball and swimming are included to guide you.

Key Components of Performance

Technical

Components	Sub-components
eg netball – individual ball skill	passing, shooting, handling

Physical

Components	Sub-components
netball – speed	reaction speed, acceleration, pure speed, agility
swimming – flexibility (backstroke)	dorsi/plantarflexion (ankles); hyper extension/flexion (lower back); posterior/anterior shoulder mobility

Tactical

Components	Sub-components
eg netball – assertive attack	awareness of game plan, variety, adaptability, options, timing
eg swimming – energy conservation	selection of leg kick tempo, target time, pacing strategy

Mental

Components	Sub-components
eg netball – decision making	speed of thought, calmness, awareness, selection of option, prioritisation
eg swimming – self-confidence	self-belief, positive thoughts, high commitment, strong focus

Now turn over.

This activity required you to draw on your knowledge of sport physiology, psychology and biomechanics, as well as the technical and tactical aspects of your sport. It may have helped you to identify some areas in which you need to improve or refresh your knowledge. Perhaps you are unsure of the latest tactical or technical variations in your sport? The Recap and What Next? section at the end of this chapter directs you to sources of further information.

2.3 Assessment of Your Performer/Team

Having identified the important components of performance, you will want to determine your performers' current standards in each component. Such information can be gathered in the training, laboratory or competition environment. The environment you choose will depend on the component to be assessed. All three environments have advantages and limitations for gathering information. The training and laboratory environments cannot mirror the competition environment exactly, for example, as it is difficult to recreate the levels of motivation experienced in competition for assessments in laboratories. This may have an effect on assessments of endurance, strength or even techniques.

It can be difficult to assess all the components of performance in the competitive environment, however, as they blend together into a whole that may mask small deficiencies. Is it possible to assess whether a footballer's flexibility is sufficient to minimise the potential for injury, just from watching him or her play? Is it possible to assess aerobic endurance accurately in the competitive environment of canoe slalom? Coaches will use a combination of different assessment methods, in all three environments, to gather the information they require.

Direct/Indirect Assessment

Components of performance can be assessed directly or indirectly. Aerobic endurance, for example, can be assessed directly, through measurement of the subject's VO_2max[1] in a laboratory. It may also be assessed indirectly by the Multistage Fitness Test[2] in the training environment. Concentration can only be measured indirectly, through error counts in the training or competition environment or by subjective assessment in questionnaires.

Subjective/Objective Assessments

Depending on how you gather the information, your assessment can be objective or subjective. Objective assessments are based on impartial evidence such as times or scores. Subjective assessments depend on your impression of the performance (eg you believe that the goalkeeper's clearances were an effective means of building an attack but you have no figures to prove it). Most coaches need impartial information to support their assessments of performance and so they will use some form of assessment. Performance assessments can take many forms, some of which are included in the following table:

---

1 VO_2max is a test to measure the volume of oxygen a performer consumes per minute of maximal activity. It is a valid test of aerobic endurance capacity.

2 A progressive shuttle running test to exhaustion. See the *Recap and What Next?* section at the end of this chapter.

Table 1: Methods of performance measurement

Method	Application	Examples
Notational/video analysis	This can be used to measure the efficacy of techniques/tactical decisions.	Accuracy of distribution from footballer. Service accuracy in tennis. Line-out success rates in rugby.
Biomechanical analysis	This is used to measure all aspects of the technical efficiency of a performer.	Throwing technique for a javelin competitor. Sprint technique analysis for a footballer.
Psychological testing	Mental skills and attitudes are difficult to assess directly and objectively, though indirect and subjective measures are available.	Standardised interviews, validated questionnaires (SCAT – Sport Competition Anxiety Test), behavioural observations (eg comparison of success rates in training and competition).
Sport-specific skills testing	Many sports have developed tests for specific skills. Refer to your own governing body.	Passing accuracy in football. Setting accuracy in volleyball. Free throws in basketball.
Laboratory based testing	Lab tests can assess almost any component, particularly fitness components.	VO$_2$max will measure aerobic endurance, Wingate test measures anaerobic endurance.
Field based fitness testing	Most fitness components can be assessed directly or indirectly without having to go to the laboratory.	The Multistage Fitness (bleep) Test is an indirect measure of aerobic endurance, as is blood lactate testing. The vertical jump is an indirect measure of power output.

Designing an Assessment Programme

Before implementing a programme of assessment[1], the coach must establish:

- the components of performance to assess
- the appropriate assessment for each component
- how to administer/conduct the assessment
- how to evaluate/interpret test results.

---

1 For further information on designing a fitness testing programme, you are referred to the **scUK** workshop *Field-based Fitness Testing* and the resource *A Guide to Field Based Fitness Testing*, complimentary with the workshop or available from **Coachwise 1st4sport** (tel 0113-201 5555 or visit www.1st4sport.com).

What components to assess

A coach will want as much relevant and accurate information as possible. However, common sense dictates that testing should not take up too much training time. As coach, you must decide which components are necessary to test, and which would be nice to test. Plan your programme of assessment around this decision. Some components may be assessed easily and inexpensively. Others are difficult to assess accurately or are expensive. This will also be an important consideration in planning your programme of testing.

What assessments to use

Assessments can provide good quality, useful information but must be selected based on a systematic approach. To ensure an assessment is providing quality information on which you can depend, it must be valid, reliable and objective.

Validity

Validity is a complex concept. It means the appropriateness, meaningfulness and usefulness of the specific inferences made from the test scores. In simple terms, when an assessment is valid, the assumption is made that the results allow you to draw conclusions about the performance status (eg fitness, mental, technical) of your performer. For example, a test of absolute strength such as a one rep maximum (1RM – the amount of weight that can be lifted once only) on a bench press might be an inappropriate assessment for a gymnast. If it were calculated in terms of a strength/weight ratio then the result would be more meaningful.

Reliability

The reliability of an assessment refers to the consistency of results over a number of tests:

- on the same occasion (repeatability)
- on different occasions (reproducibility).

Imagine the disparity of results if a twelve minute run were performed on dry firm grass in the summertime, and on a wet muddy surface in winter.

Objectivity

This is a measure of the degree of agreement between two or more different assessors on a particular assessment. Objectivity is desirable to permit different assessors to conduct the same assessment and produce similar or preferably identical results. It can be difficult for two people to administer skinfold calipers in an identical manner, for example. Objectivity is very important in fitness testing and can be increased by using:

- accurate electronic timing or measuring devices which eliminate human error

- clearly defined and strictly enforced criteria (eg when using the Multistage Fitness Test it is important to stop performers if they miss the bleep on two consecutive turns).

Laboratory versus field tests

Many coaches believe that laboratory tests are of more benefit than field-based tests, because they are more accurate and control more of the variables, and so should be more reliable. These factors must be weighed against others such as the difficulty of reproducing the demands of the sport situation in the laboratory (lack of specificity), the possible influence of an alien environment on motivation and the expense and logistical difficulties of using a laboratory. There are arguments for and against both. The test you select should be the one which best suits your needs.

Finding the right test

Using a test which has been developed for the specific component you wish to assess is usually better than inventing your own. Tests that have been professionally developed have addressed the issues of validity and reliability. Your governing body should assist you in searching for appropriate tests. Alternatively, BASES (the British Association of Sport and Exercise Sciences) will direct you to an individual qualified in the appropriate field. See the *Recap and What Next?* section at the end of this chapter for details of publications that will include references to tests and testing procedures and directions to BASES.[1]

ACTIVITY 6

Enter the preferred method of assessment for all the performance components you have identified in Activity 5. If you do not intend to assess a component, draw a line through the box. Examples are given for some assessments:

Component	Assessment method	Assessment venue		
		Laboratory	Field	Competition
Endurance	Multistage Fitness Test		✓	
Speed	30 metre sprint		✓	
Concentration	TAIS (Nideffer 1976)	✓		

---

1 For a list of accredited sport and exercise scientists you should contact **The British Association of Sport and Exercise Sciences (BASES)**, Chelsea Close, Off Amberley Road, Armley, Leeds LS12 4HP. Tel: 0113-289 1020 Website: www.bases.org.uk

Sports coaches often have a narrow perspective on testing, which usually focuses on fitness testing or technical assessments. However, there is a large number of tests available for almost every performance component. Most coaches know how and when to use fitness tests and some are aware of the potential of mental skills assessments and biomechanical assessments. Other areas, such as nutritional assessments and medical screening, are often neglected. These can highlight any factors which may predispose the performer to an increased risk of injury and illness, either during competition or training.

Medical tests can help to quantify the stresses your performer is likely to endure during training or competition, or whether your performer's anatomical structure is able to cope with the imposed stresses of competition/training. They can identify whether or not the performer has any contra-indications to exercise or sport.

A dietary assessment can provide a detailed insight into nutritional practices and help assess:

- the adequacy of the diet in terms of overall energy or specific nutrients[1]

- how to plan menus around lifestyle (eg shift/night workers, early morning training)

- whether any specific dietary manipulation is required (eg weight loss or gain).

The essential requirements of an effective nutritional assessment and subsequent nutrition plan are that they are sport-specific and tailored to your performer's needs.

Notational and video analysis

Competitions can be used to gather information on the current state of preparation of a performer or team. In many sports (such as the field games) a coach may need to use the competitive situation to gather information that cannot be gathered in training, because of the difficulty in simulating opposition. However, because of the complexity of many games, an objective measurement of some components of performance is often very difficult to obtain. How can a team's defensive performance be analysed objectively, for example? In these circumstances a coach must seek indicators based on individual elements of performance such as tackles made or possession turnovers, which can be measured and documented. Video analysis and notational analysis techniques allow the coach to focus on one aspect of performance and gather information on it.

The information generated through video or notational analysis is vital to the profiling of individual players and teams and so will provide a lot of the information that a coach will require before planning or adjusting training programmes. It can be used to identify strengths and weaknesses and measure them objectively. This enables the coach to make judgements which are based on facts and figures, and to rely less on subjective assessments of the situation.

Gathering this information can be a laborious process. There are a number of options available to the coach when this information is required. The use of notational analysis sheets is the most accessible form of match or game analysis. These may be filled out while the game or match is in progress. Usually this task can be delegated to trusted assistants or panel members. It can be difficult to keep up with the pace of play, so keep record sheets simple and if necessary, waterproof.

---

1   A substance that provides nourishment for the maintenance of life (eg very low calcium intake).

It is sometimes more desirable to perform the analysis yourself, and in this case the use of a video is essential. It is not possible to maintain the *big-picture* perspective a coach will need while concentrating on a particular aspect of analysis – it must be done after the event. Software programmes are available for many of the more popular sports which can allow you to create different permutations of the information gathered to give specific feedback. These are useful, if expensive tools.

In team games, notational and video analysis have become key mechanisms for the analysis of the performance of selves and opponents. Notational analysis can focus on team performance or on individuals. Most coaches choose to draft their own notational analysis sheets, so the information they acquire is tailored to their own needs.

When compiling a match analysis sheet:

- identify the component of performance you want to analyse/measure
- decide on the specific criteria you will use to measure that component
- determine the exact parameters you will use to define these criteria
- decide how these criteria will be recorded
- ensure that the recording process is as simple as possible and manageable in real time.

For example, a rugby coach might decide, in accordance with the above procedure:

- I want to analyse turnovers of our possession to attempt to identify patterns
- a turnover occurs if possession changes hands without a score occurring
- turnovers may occur in open play, if we take the ball out of play or if a scrum is awarded to the opposition from our possession
- this process will be recorded by my assistant coach during the game.

Set play	Position on pitch	First phase play	No of phases	Player losing possession	Reason for loss
Kick-off	B3	Kick to box	1	9	Kick too long
Line-out	C3	Kick to touch	1	10	Safety play
Line-out	B3	Strike channel 1(12)	4	2	Poor body pos in tackle

Such information could provide the coach with objective feedback on the patterns and reasons for his team losing possession. It would allow him to give feedback to his players and to pinpoint specific problems. Examples of other match analysis sheets for rugby union follow – the same principles apply to other sports:

Scrums to Leicester

Zone	Back/Wheel Forward/Stable/Penalty/Free Kick	Push Over	Backs						Kicks				Ball Carrier	Success/Fail
			Move Left	Move Right	CH1	CH2	CH3	Blind Side	Tough	High	Position	Drop	Behind Defence	

Line-out to Leicester

Zone	No of Men	Throw to	F. Kick Won/Lost/Void/Penalty	Maul/CT/Def/Ruck/Loose	Used by Forwards	Kick				Backs			Success/Fail
						Tough	High	Position	Drop	C1	C2	C3	

Figure 3: Match analysis sheets for rugby union

2.4 Analysing and Interpreting Results

Gathering the information is often the easy part of evaluating performance. The information must be interpreted and a judgement made on the performer or team, based on that information. Although the process of analysing and interpreting the results of valid and reliable assessments may appear fairly straightforward, subjective judgements often need to be made on the basis of the information collected.

There are a multitude of factors which affect performance in tests, only some of which are controllable by the tester. Factors such as motivation and anxiety can cause the results to vary considerably. It is important to remember that the results of tests are very much secondary to the performance in competition. An undue emphasis on the performance in tests can be anxiety-inducing in the athlete and coach.

One of the most important aspects of assessments is the *perception of the result by the performer.* Therefore it is vital to give positive feedback to your performers about any tests carried out. The way in which the information gathered is analysed and fed back to the performer will determine whether it has a positive or negative effect on motivation.

ACTIVITY 7

Jot down any factors that might affect a performer's perceptions of test results:

-

-

-

Now turn over.

You may have thought of:

- *the coach's opinion or perception of the scores*
- *other performers' opinions or perception of the scores*
- *the score in relation to the performer's specific goals and more general aspirations.*

Although the test results are an objective set of measurements, they will be interpreted against a background of expectations based on your performer's goals and aspirations. The training completed prior to the testing will provide a frame for the performer's perception of the results.

The performers' rationalisation of the test results can provide an insight into the state of their self-confidence. Both positive and negative results can be attributed to internal (I felt good today/felt poorly today) or external factors (I ate the wrong food this morning/I never do well at this track!). In general, elite performers (because they tend to have high levels of self-confidence) attribute blame for poor results to external factors, and assume the credit for good results themselves. This is a mechanism to protect their self-confidence. If their reasoning is contrary to this, it may be worth investigating.

The coach will interpret the scores in relation to past experience and other performers will tend to compare results with their own. For your performer(s), the interpretation of the results will depend on a combination of their own expectations and their perceptions of other people's reactions.

The impact that assessments have on training programme design should now be very apparent. You can use the information gathered as baseline information on which you will plan your performers' programmes of preparation. You will also want to use many of the same assessments to set goals and monitor your performers' progress towards their goals. This will be discussed in Chapter Seven (Monitoring Progress). If you need help with the design and implementation of assessment programmes, it may be beneficial for you to contact a sport scientist who could help you with more complex procedures.

2.5 Recap and What Next?

This chapter has encouraged you to outline the specific demands of your sport. This is a very necessary process for all coaches, so that training programmes are as complete as possible and leave nothing to chance.

It is important to examine your performer(s) in the context of these demands. Performer assessment is the first step in the planning of coaching programmes. Chapter Three will help you to use performance profiling to ensure that the programme of preparation you plan is concurrent with your performers' or team's perceptions of their needs.

The following packs may be useful in attempting to profile the demands of your sport. They are available from **Coachwise 1st4sport** (0113-201 5555).

Brewer, J, Ramsbottom, R and Williams, C (1998) **Multistage fitness test.** 2nd edition. Leeds, National Coaching Foundation. ISBN 0 902523 06 7.

Davis, J (1996) **Fitness for games players.** Leeds, National Coaching Foundation, ISBN 0 947850 10 4.

Farrally, M (1996) **An introduction to sports physiology.** 2nd edition. Leeds, National Coaching Foundation. ISBN 0 947850 96 1.

Farrally, M (1995) **An introduction to the structure of the body.** 2nd edition. Leeds, National Coaching Foundation and Scottish Sports Council. ISBN 1 902523 49 0.

National Coaching Foundation (1997) **Physiology and performance.** 3rd edition. Leeds, National Coaching Foundation. ISBN 0 947850 24 4.

Sellars, C (1996) **Mental skills: an introduction for sports coaches.** Leeds, National Coaching Foundation. ISBN 0 947850 34 1.

Wilkinson, D and Moore, P (1995) **A guide to field based fitness testing.** Leeds, National Coaching Foundation, ISBN 0 947850 55 4.

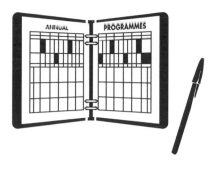

CHAPTER THREE
Profiling Needs and Action Planning

3.0 What's in It for You?

Programmes of preparation, to be effective, must be relevant, realistic and accepted by your performers. This chapter will help you to plan programmes that fit these requirements.

Coaches frequently encounter problems with performer motivation, failure to listen and poor attitude to training – these are often created when coach and performer have different perceptions of the performer's priorities and abilities. Many coaches use *performance profiling* to help them understand how their performers perceive themselves and their performances. This tool can ensure that both you and your performers are working to the same agenda.

Goal-setting turns the agenda that you create in the profiling exercise into action steps. By basing your goal-setting practices on a performance profile, you are assured the goals you set with your performers are relevant to them and that your carefully constructed programme is realistic and accepted by the performer.

By the end of this chapter you will be able to:

- explain performance profiling

- use performance profiling to generate a profile of your performers/team

- use goal-setting to focus your preparation programmes on performer needs.

3.1 Performance Profiling

Performance profiling[1] generates a profile of your performer/team's performance against the performance components that produce a top performance in your sport. It is a tool to help you as a coach to understand your performers' perceptions of their strengths and weaknesses. This information can then be used to identify discrepancies between your perceptions and your performers' perceptions of how they are performing.

Performance profiling is a useful exercise for ensuring that performer and coach are working to the same agenda. It may also be used to prioritise performance components in the planning of training programmes, and can be a useful mechanism for monitoring progress towards a performer's or team's goals.

Performance Profiling in Team Sports

Coaches in team sports will want to complete the profiling exercise at two levels. They will profile their team to generate a collective perspective on strengths and weaknesses. This can be a powerful tool for ensuring that the team are on the same wavelength and share the same philosophy. The exercise can also identify the team's perceptions of their ability to use different game plans and tactics, which can often be different from that of the coach.

---

1   Further details can be found in *Performance Profiling*, available from **Coachwise 1st4sport** (tel 0113-201 5555 or visit www.1st4sport.com).

Team coaches might also profile each individual within their squads. All players will have perceptions about their strengths and weaknesses, which may or may not be in line with those of the coach. Disagreements on selection policy and training programme content can be minimised if coaches understand players' perception of their performances.

Creating the individual profile

There are some important procedural steps to follow when completing a performance profile. The process is led by the performer, and requires him/her to:

1   generate qualities which describe a top performance
    It is important that these qualities are generated by the performer without any direction. Some assistance may be needed in clarifying his or her thoughts, but the coach should not lead the discussion.

2   clarify exactly what is meant by each quality
    It is easy to misconstrue a performer's meaning, or to impose your own interpretation on a term the performer is using in a different context.

3   rate him/herself on these qualities from one to ten
    Again the performer must rate him or herself without any assistance from the coach. Ten should represent the highest level which the performer believes is achievable.

4   plot the scores on the profile chart

5   using the same scale, plot where he/she would like to be in twelve months
    This should be used as an indication of the performer's priorities.

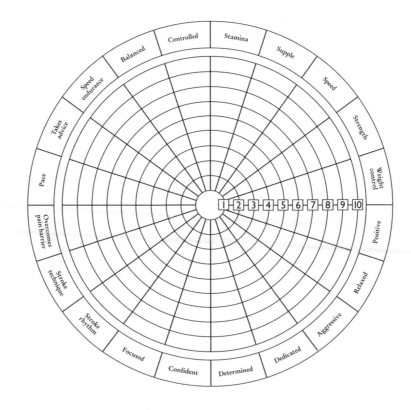

Figure 4: Profiling chart generated by a swimmer

ACTIVITY 8

1 Ask your performer to select the 20 most important qualities required to achieve a top performance in your sport. Write them in the space below. There is no need to rank them.

2 Transfer the 20 qualities listed in the previous exercise to the perimeter of the following blank profile (if repeating the exercise with different performers, use a separate profile for each one). Use the example of the swimmer as a guide. (Refer to Appendix A where a full page version is available.)

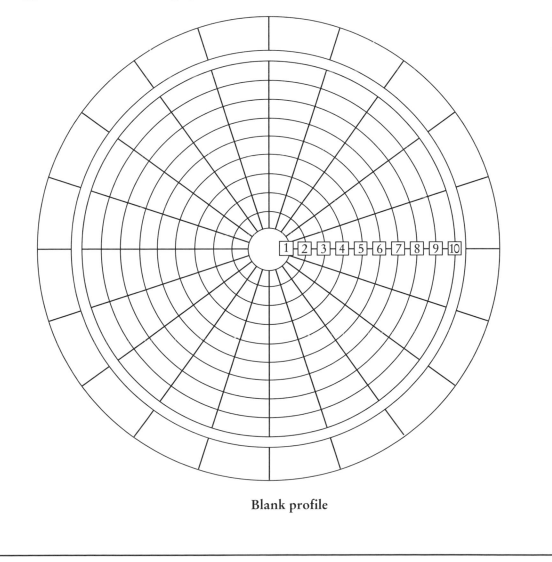

Blank profile

ACTIVITY 9

Now your performer should rate him or herself on a rating scale (1 to 10) for each quality, as shown:

Not at all   Very much

　　1　　　2　　　3　　　4　　　5　　　6　　　7　　　8　　　9　　　10

Two guidelines help in using the rating scale:

- Do not spend too long analysing each quality, trust your first impression or feeling.
- When profiling, try to use the whole range of the scale.

Use the rating scale to score each quality and mark these scores on Profile 1 on Page 31. Figure 5 provides an example of this.

Figure 5: Profile of a netball goal keeper

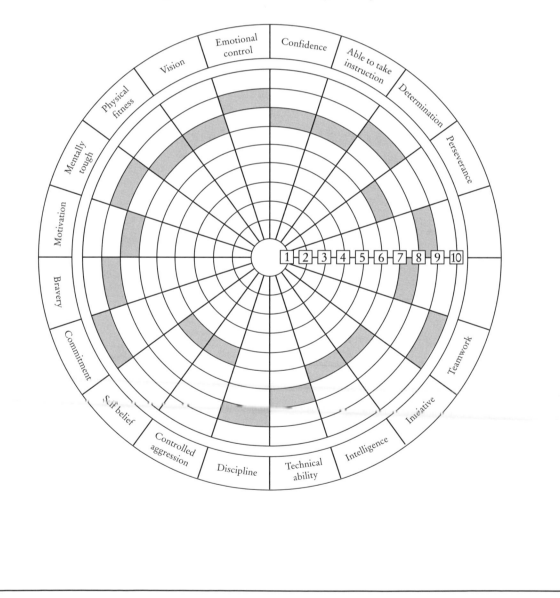

The example below is a performance profile generated by a swimmer.

*The completed profile will now highlight those qualities which the performer believes to be strong aspects of his or her overall performance. In Figure 5, the performer considers herself to be strong on the quality **commitment**.*

*It has also highlighted the weak areas and will provide the basis for structuring a training programme to help this player improve in these areas. In Figure 5, the weak areas were identified as **controlled aggression** and **self-belief**.*

3.2 Team Profiling

The reasons for completing a team profile are very similar to those for the individual profile. The problem lies in the generation of a common consensus from a large number of individuals on their self-perceptions. This process is an important step in team-building, so teams that are in a later stage of development – that have played together for some time – should find the process easier. The activity should accelerate the team-building process in a developing team by providing a shared understanding of the important qualities for team performance and by enhancing their self awareness as a group of people with a common set of goals. The following steps are a suggestion for introducing the activity, but you may wish to adjust them to suit your team and circumstances.

1   Generate the qualities the team believe to be important for team success. Bear in mind the characteristics of a top team in your sport, as well as your own team when it is successful. This is best completed in an open brainstorming session where all contributions are valid and noted.

2   Clarify what is meant by each quality.

3   Individuals rank the top five qualities they believe to be the most important for their team's success (rank one being the most important).

4   The qualities are assigned points according to how they have been ranked (each first rank is worth five points, down to the fifth rank which is worth one point).

5   The ten qualities with the most points are used for the profiling exercise and written in the chart.

6   Individuals rate the team from 0–10 for each quality.

7   The average score is marked on the profile as the team rating for that quality.

This exercise is an easy one to perform and can remove the guesswork from the coach's task of assessing the mood and confidence of the team. It is important that the profiling is completed honestly. The coach must make it clear that individuals can make an honest and open contribution.

Team Performance Profile

	Qualities	1	2	3	4	5	6	7	8	9	10

Key Issues in Profiling

It is important to appreciate that when you profile performers and teams you are dealing with their perceptions of the requirements for top performance and their perceptions of their own performances in relation to these requirements. These may or may not be concurrent with your perceptions. Any gap between your perceptions and your performer's perceptions can create problems with a programme of preparation.

Consider the shooter's coach who discovered that among the qualities the shooter identified as characterising top performance was *alley-cat syndrome*. What does it mean? How do you coach it? Without the performance profiling exercise this particular aspect of performance would not have been addressed by the coach – he did not know what it meant. Yet the performer obviously felt it was crucial. There was a disparity between his perceptions and that of his coach. Whether this disparity was semantic or whether it went deeper was something the coach had to discover through a process of discussion with the performer.

Consider also the boxer whose self-ratings for all the different components of performance were three to four points higher than his coach's ratings. Why would that disparity occur? How does one deal with that in planning coaching programmes?

There is no correct answer to the questions that the profiling exercise raises. The disparities in perception are the basis for a process of negotiation between the performer(s) and the coach. That negotiation should lead to an improved understanding and a shared perspective on performances and preparation for performance. This shared understanding can then form the basis for the joint planning of a comprehensive programme of preparation. This usually begins with a goal-setting process.

Using profiling to prioritise training

It is common practice for coaches to work on a performer's weaknesses in preparation for competition but as the competition approaches to spend the final preparation period reinforcing strengths. This will increase the likelihood of the performer being in a positive state of mind about the contest. The performance profiling exercise is a key component of that aspect of training. Not only does it give the coach an indication of the best areas to concentrate on prior to competition, it provides him or her with a record of the performer or team's perceptions of changes in the profile as the competition approaches. If the profile did not show an improvement in the performer's ratings for his or her strengths and weaknesses, then there is obviously some doubt about the thoroughness of the preparation. It is then unlikely the performer is in the optimal state of mind for competition. That would need to be addressed as a matter of priority.

3.3 Setting Goals

In the assessment of your performers and the profiling exercise, you have generated a lot of information about your performers. This information provides you with the foundation on which to plan your programmes of preparation.

The programme of assessment has informed the profiling exercise. The profiling exercise and subsequent discussions with your performer or team has generated a consensus on the areas of relative strength and weakness. This will enable you and your performers to prioritise the components of performance in your programme of preparation. The profiling exercise therefore provides a platform from which to launch your planning of the specific areas in your programme.

You will want to improve performance in the areas you and your performer have prioritised. In order to provide a focus for this work you will require clear and meaningful goals. These goals will ensure the programmes are coordinated and relevant. Goals can increase your performers' commitment to their training programmes. It has been demonstrated that the motivation of performers will be enhanced if they have achievable goals to work towards, and if they have set these goals for themselves.

The next section will remind you of the important issues when setting goals with your performers. Use the exercises that follow to hone your goal-setting skills. When you set goals for real, remember they must be set jointly by coach and performer.

Principles of Goal-setting

A goal is the aim or object of your endeavours. For sportspeople, goals are the framework on which preparation for competition is constructed. Goals, to be effective, should conform to the basic principles outlined in the following panel.

All goals should be **SMART** – they should be:

S pecific   it is difficult to assess the success of vague goals

M easurable   quantifiable goals can be measured and assessed

A greed   goals agreed by the participants and coach

R ealistic   goals should be challenging but within the performer's capability

T ime-phased each goal should have a specified time-scale in which to be achieved[1].

Identifying SMART goals is easier in some sports than others. For example, specific, measurable goals are easier to identify when performance can be directly measured (eg long jump), timed (eg swimming) or scored (eg archery). However, with practice and ingenuity, appropriate and quantifiable goals can be set for any sport (eg numbers of turn overs or rebounds in basketball, number of errors on the backhand in badminton, time taken between points in tennis). Sport psychologists have shown that higher levels of performance occur when the goals set are more specific and difficult. Goals which are set **for** the performer, rather than **by** or **with** the performer, are unlikely to be as well accepted and are therefore less likely to be achieved.

ACTIVITY 10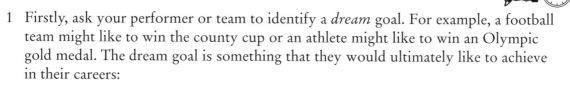

1 Firstly, ask your performer or team to identify a *dream* goal. For example, a football team might like to win the county cup or an athlete might like to win an Olympic gold medal. The dream goal is something that they would ultimately like to achieve in their careers:

2 For the areas prioritised in the performer's profile, set three long-term goals (eg over a season) that will contribute towards achieving the dream goal (make sure each goal is a SMART goal):

-

-

-

Now turn over.

---

1 If you require more information on goal-setting, you are referred to Chapter 2 of **scUK**'s resource *Mental Skills: An Introduction for Sports Coaches.* Available from **Coachwise 1st4sport** (tel 0113-201 5555 or visit www.1st4sport.com).

As an illustration, the swimmer profiled in Figure 4 (page 30) has a dream goal of winning the national championships in two years. On discussion with his coach, they identified the winning time in the nationals for the previous two years and set a goal based on achieving that time in competition.

In the performance profile, the weak areas were the psychological areas of focus, relaxation and control. The swimmer set himself a long-term goal for the last meet of the season (nationals) – that he would remain relaxed and focused throughout the lead up to the event and the race itself. His coach agreed that this was achievable. They also agreed on a state anxiety scale questionnaire that they would use as a tool to help them monitor progress in this area. In this way the goal became measurable.

However, they were not close to achieving this goal. It was necessary to set some intermediate goals that would allow coach and performer to track progress towards the long-term goal. Swimmer and coach agreed that controlling thought content in the lead up to the race and the race itself was the most important skill to develop. The coach identified the technical factors that were most important in each section of the race and a race strategy for thought content was developed based on these.

Intermediate goals were set for the swimmer to concentrate on a certain aspect of stroke technique for each split. These goals were staggered through the following months, so that for the first month the swimmer was attempting to maintain concentration on a specific area of technique for 200m; in the following month he practised switching focus to another factor for the next 200m and so on.

Other intermediate goals were set which worked towards developing a strong and adaptable pre-race strategy. This again focused on controlling thought content by setting a time schedule for mental and physical routines before the race.

Short-term goals were set for the next competition. The swimmer agreed to log thought patterns in the period leading up to the race and during the race. This would serve as a baseline for further short-term goal-setting, moving towards the first set of intermediate goals.

Setting Team Goals

While it is obvious that each individual within a team will set goals for his or her individual training programme, it is also important that team goals are set. This will be an important part of developing team spirit, as well as providing a framework for the development of team skills, tactics and match plans. Team goal-setting is rather more difficult than for individuals, but is just as important. Goals for the team should be set communally and democratically (if they are to be accepted), though as coach you will want to have a significant input. Team meetings at the beginning of the training year are important forums for the setting of such goals and targets.

3.4 Types of Goals

Goals tied directly to an outcome are said to have an outcome orientation. Examples of **outcome goals** can be:

- coming first
- winning a medal
- making a final
- being selected for a team.

This type of goal can be affected by the performance of others and therefore is not completely under the control of the performer. For example, a hockey coach should be wary if her team sets a target of winning 75% of the games in a season. This goal could become self-defeating because it may be outside the performers' control to achieve it. Player's self-confidence may be affected if goals they have committed themselves to become obviously unachievable in mid season.

Process goals specify what needs to be done in order to be successful and usually refer to an element of performance. They may not conform to SMART principles. An example of a process goal for a tennis player might be to concentrate on the placement of the toss for every serve. This would help the performer to achieve a specific performance goal relating to service accuracy. Process goals are directly under the performer's control.

Goals which focus on the quality of performance are generally more controllable as they are not compared with others or directly influenced by someone else's performance. They can be readily stated in specific, measurable terms and provide for an absolute benchmark of performance such as time, distance or personal score.

It is generally better if you set goals related to performance, though often outcome goals can be effective long-term motivational tools – do not dismiss them out of hand. Treat them with caution and try to ensure that when they are used, they will be achieved. Process goals are useful for performers to take into competition. They can remove the thought of the consequences of performing well or badly.

ACTIVITY II

Turn back to Activity Ten (page 36) and assess whether the goals you set were outcome or process goals.

Goal	Outcome	Process
	☐	☐
	☐	☐
	☐	☐
	☐	☐
	☐	☐
	☐	☐

Goals are the structure on which a programme of preparation can be based. If managed properly, the goal-setting process provides a framework for improving performance through the short-, medium- and long-terms. The next activity will require you to construct goals that build in this manner.

ACTIVITY 12

Based on your performer profile from Activity 8 (page 31), complete the following:

Choose a long-term *outcome* goal from the previous exercise:

- Set an intermediate-term goal that will help you to achieve this long-term goal.

- Now set short-term goals that will help you to achieve this intermediate-term goal.

    -

    -

    -

- Set a *process* goal that will be relevant to achieving one of these outcome goals:

Set these goals using the SMART principles and bear in mind the commitments of your performers, their situations, needs and other aspirations within the sport.

You will come back to this activity later in the pack.

You should not have found this activity too difficult, as you have generated all the information needed to complete it. It is important that all goals are based on the SMART principles.

In some sports, like swimming and running, far more time is spent training than competing – it is therefore vital that your performers get the most out of every training session. Set goals for each training session with your performers – this will help your performers focus on the key points of each session. For example, footballers could write a key word on a sticking plaster, such as *concentration*, and then place it on the back of their hands. During a lull in the training session, a quick glance at the plaster may encourage them to re-focus on their goals.

Recording Goals

As described earlier, goals must be recorded and agreed by both performer and coach. Committing goals to paper has been shown to increase adherence to the goals. A goal-setting contract should be designed by the performer (this contract should be between the performer and him or herself – not between performer and coach). This contract could be kept by the performer or the coach, whatever the preference of the performer, and be available for updating at regular intervals. A performer's training diary is a useful place to record goals.

It is usual to build and record goals around planning units. Long-term goals will be formed in the context of important events (major competitions) and medium- and short-term goals will have shorter time-scales (a season or shorter cycle).

Your goal-setting process may be as elaborate or as simple as you like. Often this will depend on the preferences of your performer. It is important that a similar process for goal-setting is used from season to season, so your performer may become familiar with it.

3.5 Recap and What Next?

The performer assessments, the performance profile and the goal-setting exercise have generated the information needed to form the basis of your long-term training plan. The next chapter will investigate the process of adaptation to training stresses and you will begin to divide the training/competitive season into its smaller constituent parts.

The following packs, which are available from **Coachwise 1st4sport** (0113-201 5555) will complement the information in this chapter:

Butler, R (1996) **Performance profiling**. (Tape and booklet) Leeds, National Coaching Foundation. ISBN 0 947850 36 8.

Cabral, P and Crisfield, P (1999) **Motivation and mental toughness.** 2nd edition. Leeds, National Coaching Foundation. ISBN 0 902523 24 5.

Hardy, L and Fazey, J (1990) **Goal-setting.** (Tape and booklet) Leeds, National Coaching Foundation. ISBN 0 947850 69 4.

Sellars, C (1996) **Mental skills: an introduction for sports coaches.** Leeds, National Coaching Foundation. ISBN 0 947850 34 1.

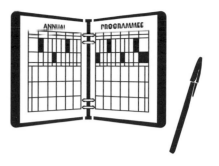

CHAPTER FOUR
Adaptation and Training Principles

4.0 What's in It for You?

The goal-setting process outlined in Chapter Three provides the framework on which your preparation for performance is constructed. To achieve the goals you and your performer have set, training programmes must be designed for every component of performance. If these programmes are to be effective, they must facilitate the process of adaptation.

Under the right conditions, the body and mind will react to the stresses imposed in training by increasing their capacity to cope with such stress. This is the process of adaptation and it explains the training effect. The coach's task is to create the right conditions for optimal adaptation to occur.

The process of adaptation is governed by the principles of training. These principles apply to all the components of performance – whether physical, technical, tactical or mental. Programmes of training are constructed by applying the principles of training to the components of performance.

By the end of this chapter, you should be able to:

- explain the physiology and psychology of the adaptation process
- outline the principles of training
- construct training programmes for individual components of performance to help your performers achieve the goals they have set.

4.1 Principles of Training

The major objective in training is to facilitate physical and psychological adaptations so that performance will be improved in specific tasks. These adaptations are governed by specific principles which are as follows:

Individual differences
Different people will react to training in different ways.

Adaptation
The body and mind adapt to training stress by increasing their ability to cope with such stresses.

Overload
For optimal effect, the training load must exceed that normally experienced by the performer.

Reversibility
Training effects will be lost if they are not maintained by a programme of training.

Specificity
The adaptation brought on by training will be specific to the type of training undertaken.

Progression
The training load should be progressively increased to account for the increased capacity of the performer.

Variation
Training should be varied, as constant training of the same type will lead to a stage of diminishing returns.

Recovery
Recovery becomes increasingly important as training volume increases. As performers develop, more components of performance are added to their programme and their training load in each increases. Recovery then becomes a vital aspect of preparation.

In addition to recovery, the most important of these principles for planning purposes are **specificity, progression, reversibility.** If you are familiar with the principles which govern adaptation, you will be able to apply these to your athletes' training programmes, thus ensuring they get maximum benefit from their training time. The next activity will allow you to evaluate your knowledge in this area.

ACTIVITY 13

Without reference to any other source, try to define the following principles of training and explain them by drawing upon a specific example from your own sport:

Specificity

eg

Overload

eg

Reversibility

eg

Now turn over.

Carefully read through the following explanations to see how much you have remembered. You might wish to highlight anything you omitted. Additional principles will also be discussed.

Specificity

All adaptation is highly specific. In other words, adaptation will occur to the specific loads or stresses which are placed on the performer. Consequently, to improve passing skills under pressure, a performer must practise under limited conditions of time and space; to improve aerobic fitness, the aerobic system must be worked; to help athletes cope with the stress imposed by an audience, they need to develop coping skills and be given opportunities to practise in front of an audience. Adaptations in all these areas will be specific to the activity performed in training. For example, a performer who has developed a high maximal oxygen uptake in running will not necessarily have a similar level when different muscle groups are exercised, as in swimming and rowing. A footballer who has developed a high level of confidence in his passing ability will not necessarily approach a situation where he must shoot for goal with the same level of confidence.

Overload

If the training session is to have the desired effect, the demand of the particular activity must be greater than those with which the performer can comfortably cope. Achieving the appropriate training load for each person is important. Too much can cause pain, injury and ultimately overtraining or burn-out. Too little will mean no gain.

Achieving the appropriate overload requires the skilful manipulation of training **volume** and **intensity**. The volume of your training will be determined by the frequency and duration of your training sessions. The intensity of your training sessions is a measure of how close to your maximum ability you are performing. These three variables (frequency, intensity and time/duration – often called the **FIT** principles[1]) will determine the training overload.

Balancing training volume and intensity is very important. Athletes are not able to maintain workloads of high intensity for long periods of time, and yet will want to be training at a maximum intensity as competition approaches. For example, in terms of strength or weight training, the volume of training is determined by the number of exercises, sets and repetitions performed per session (duration) and how often the sessions occur (frequency). The intensity of training depends on the percentage of the athlete's maximum lift he is lifting. To achieve the appropriate overload you would manipulate the number of exercises, resistance, number of repetitions or the number of sessions per week.

In mental and technical training, an overload on the performer's concentration levels might require the coach to increase the number of potential distractions. A rugby goalkicker might practise his goalkicking skills on a busy training pitch, or with a number of distractions created by other players.

---

1   If these principles are new to you or you would like to refresh your memory, you are referred to the **scUK** workshop *Fitness and Training* and the resource *Physiology and Performance*, complimentary with the workshop or available from **Coachwise 1st4sport** (tel 0113-201 5555 or visit www.1st4sport.com).

Progression

As a performer's capacity increases through training, greater demands must be made if improvements are to continue. For example, a tennis player receiving serve may be at a stage of development where it is possible to judge how a serve will bounce only after it has hit the ground. The coach might gradually increase the number of cues[1] to be attended to (for example, where the opponent tosses the ball and how the swing progresses) until the performer is capable of monitoring the whole action of the serve and returning more effectively.

Reversibility

This means *if you don't use it, you lose it.* If the training load is reduced or stopped completely, the level of adaptation gained will start to drop. In general, **slow gain** training methods (where the component is improved slowly) imply slow loss when training load is cut. Conversely, **fast gain** methods (eg crash fitness programmes) imply quick loss when the training is reduced. This means that all performers should train regularly and they should follow maintenance programmes in those areas of performance that are not prioritised for the current training period.

Recovery

The relationship between loading and recovery is also vital. Rest is perhaps the most important training principle and heavy training sessions should be followed by lighter ones or even total rest. This allows the body to adapt to the stress being placed on it. It is important to remember that the training effect comes during the activity itself for tactical, technical and mental training, but during the recovery period for physical training. For example, after a strength training session, energy stores are replenished and damaged tissue is repaired or replaced. It is essential that sufficient rest is allowed between training units for this recuperation and replenishment to take place. The more intense the training, the longer the recovery required.

It should not be assumed that recovery means complete rest or inactivity. A swimmer for example, may work on aerobic endurance in the morning and could recover in the evening by working on basic speed and stroke technique. In Chapter Six you will be shown how to integrate and balance the various performance qualities to provide optimal improvement. *Overtraining* can occur when insufficient time is allowed for recovery – this will be discussed in more detail in the next section.

Now check the accuracy of your responses to the previous activity. Specificity, overload and reversibility are important principles to remember in relation to technical, mental, tactical and physical training. However, mental, tactical and technical training are not often considered in terms of the principles of training. Ensure you have grasped these fully before reading on.

---

1   A signal or stimulus resulting in a desired behaviour or action depending on the circumstances.

4.2 The Process of Adaptation

Training results in physical or mental changes to a performer. These changes occur throughout the training period even though there may not be an obvious and immediate improvement. It takes time to adapt to the training load. Repeated loading and fatigue situations are necessary stimuli for adaptations to occur. Therefore, the interplay between loading, recovery, training intensity and training volume is vital.

The Overcompensation Model

During a training session, performers begin to experience fatigue and, if they continued for some time, they would be unable to continue at the same intensity. For example, they might no longer be able to maintain the required concentration or lift the same weight. They would be unable to repeat the training session just undertaken. During the following recovery period, the adaptations to that training load occur. This process of adaptation is referred to as **super** or **overcompensation** (Figure 6).

Loading, recovery and overcompensation are the keys to effective training. Training causes fatigue and a temporary reduction in performance. Improvement occurs during the recovery phase when the overcompensation takes place. Following this compensation, the performer is able to train at a higher level (eg maintain concentration for longer, lift heavier weights, produce more accurate serves). It is important to note that:

- there may be a loss or weakened training effect if the time interval between training units is too long – overcompensation will be diminished and the performer may regress to the initial level before the subsequent training load is administered

- if the training stimulus is frequently applied with adequate recovery periods, increases in physiological capacity will occur

- if the loads are applied without sufficient recovery time a chronic stress situation may occur (overtraining).

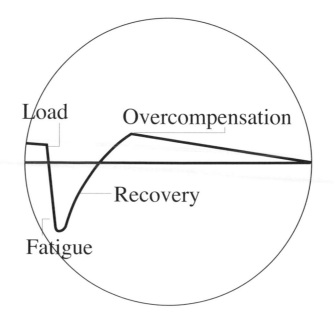

Figure 6: Model of overcompensation

The overcompensation model illustrates the effect of training and the resulting fatigue. During the recovery phase, adaptations occur within the system or systems that have been overloaded and an overcompensation phase (ie increased capacity) can occur. If the performer trains again during this period, then the overcompensation is reinforced and increased. If the performer misses training, there will be a return to the initial level (when the training effect is wasted).

Recovery

Recovery should include physiological (restoration and regeneration) and psychological procedures. There are four major methods:

- work-to-rest ratios
- nutrition
- physical therapies
- psychological skills.

Work–to–rest ratios are important both within and between training sessions; they depend on the type of work being done. For example, the recovery times between sets/intervals for strength and power development are relatively short and frequent compared with aerobic training when they are longer and less frequent. The body requires recuperative time for adaptation to occur and consequently, rest periods need to be programmed into training schedules. Sessions should be sequenced (Chapter Five) to include lighter work within the week, month or cycle to promote physical adaptation. Rest days, cross training and stretching are all forms of active rest. Psychological regeneration is promoted by providing the mind with alternate sets of stimuli. Sleep is also important. Any disruption in your performer's sleeping pattern can have detrimental effects on performance.

Nutrition should be given the same consideration as rest and recovery. The body needs enough of the right food at the right times to provide energy for exercise and essential nutrients which help repair exercised muscles – a well balanced diet is essential. A poor or inadequate diet can lead to fatigue, irritability and perhaps to eating disorders such as anorexia. Attention to the body's waste products can indicate whether your performer is eating the right sort of things and is well hydrated (eg clear, non-smelling urine is a sign of adequate hydration).

A wide range of **physical therapies** can be used to promote restoration (eg hydrotherapies, sports massage). Showers, spa baths, hot baths, float tanks, saunas and plunge pools are excellent environments to stretch and perform self massage – they increase circulation and sensory stimulation to promote physiological and psychological recovery. Rehydration is an essential part of the process so water bottles are used with these therapies to prevent dehydration. Sports massage increases blood flow and enhances the delivery of oxygen and nutrients to tired muscles, helping remove waste products. It also helps to warm and stretch soft tissues, providing temporary flexibility gains. There are also psychological benefits associated with sports massage. As tired and tight muscles relax with restoration, there is a corresponding improvement in mood states – the performer feels less fatigued and more relaxed.

Simple **psychological techniques** can provide benefits such as increased self-awareness, improved motivation and decreased reactions to stress. A strong relationship exists between physical and mental relaxation – they produce similar responses (lower heart rates and blood pressure and improved mood states). Some of the more frequently used techniques include:

- **progressive muscle relaxation** – tightening and relaxing specific muscles

- **autogenic relaxation** – self-induced technique of focusing on producing heavy and warm sensations within specific muscle groups

- **imagery relaxation** – using imagination to create a vivid scene in the mind promoting feelings of comfort and relaxation

- **breathing drills** – breathing deeply to produce a state of relaxation.

Developing performer self-monitoring programmes is an effective method of guarding against overtraining, illness and injury. Chapter Six examines ways in which your performers can monitor themselves on a daily basis and provides an effective means of detecting signs of illness, injury or overtraining. If you require further information on psychological skills refer to the *Recap and What Next?* section at the end of the chapter.

The next activity requires you to take the process of adaptation and the principles of training into account when designing a programme of training for one training component.

ACTIVITY 14

1   Select one component of performance from your team or performer's profile.

Component ....

2   Plan a six week training programme that you would use to develop this quality only. Disregard, for the present, the other demands on the performer's time and energy. Ensure the programme conforms to the principles of training as outlined in this chapter. Use the planner on the next page to assist you in structuring the programme.

3   Outline in detail the passive and active recovery periods planned in this programme.

---

6 Week Training Programme

Performer/Team: .... Component: ....

Week	Activity	Recovery
1		
2		
3		
4		
5		
6		

The ability to apply the principles of training to the development of training programmes is central to the task of the coach in any sport. The process you have completed in the last exercise must be repeated for all the components of performance. Chapter Five will assist you in merging the training programmes for the many different components.

It is important that the overall training load does not exceed the capabilities of your performer. The next section deals with the potential for overtraining and how to avoid it by careful planning and monitoring.

Overtraining

Figure 7 illustrates how the body adapts to training through the process of overcompensation. However, it is important that you understand how poor planning and a lack of control over the training principles can lead to overtraining.

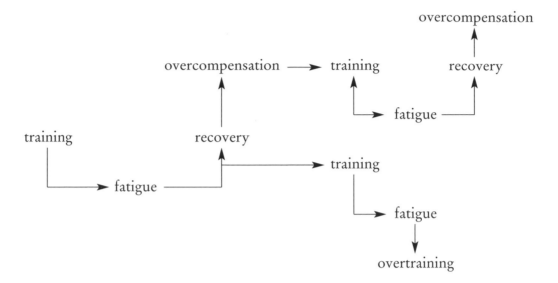

Figure 7: Overcompensation and overtraining

If the performer trains again before full recovery, overcompensation does not happen. Instead, overtraining occurs and quality of performance is reduced. In other words, if recovery is inadequate, adaptation does not occur.

The condition of **overtraining** is defined as a temporary imbalance between training and recovery, most easily noticed as fatigue that does not disappear with normal rest. As a result, performance deteriorates because the performer experiences increasing difficulty recovering from training sessions. Overtraining[1] is characterised by a complex combination of physical and mental signs and symptoms including:

- reduced performance in competition/training
- loss of weight
- loss of appetite
- muscle soreness/tenderness
- increased susceptibility to colds
- lack of motivation for training intensities
- sleeping difficulty
- slow recovery from training
- general irritability
- increased heart rate at low work
- increased resting heart rate.

1   For further information on overtraining signs and symptoms you are referred to Coaching Focus No 28, Spring 1995: *Overtraining and Fatigue*. Leeds, National Coaching Foundation. Available from **Coachwise 1st4sport** (tel 0113-201 5555 or visit www.1st4sport.com) while stocks last.

These signs will help you recognise overtraining in your performers without expert scientific or medical support. If you notice any irregular signs and symptoms in your performer, it is important you seek further advice[1] on the diagnosis and, if necessary, management of the condition.

The difficulty, of course, is that every individual is unique and work intensities and recovery periods for one performer will not necessarily work for another. This creates problems for coaches training teams and squads. It is inappropriate to work from a team or squad programme that does not take account of individual differences. Many team coaches stream their players into different groups to overcome this obstacle. Athletics or swimming squad members may work on different training programmes at the same time, in adjacent lanes.

Each performer will be affected by different environmental factors (eg social pressure, work, employment, education, family) and these factors, if not managed correctly, will have a detrimental effect on performance. Figure 8 illustrates the relationships between training, performance and lifestyle management.

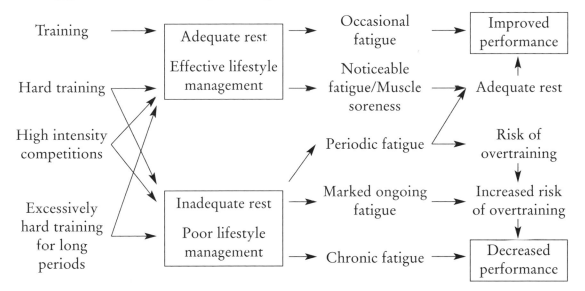

Figure 8: Interrelationships between training, fatigue, overtraining and lifestyle, adapted from Martin & Coe[2]

It should be very clear that it is not only excessive training loads which lead to overtraining. The training programme may be well within your performer's limits; however, the sum of all the other demands on your performer (lifestyle etc) can compete with the amount of energy available to train and compete. It is important to monitor your performers and encourage them to monitor themselves for overtraining or chronic fatigue. Some useful procedures for this are outlined in Chapter Six.

---

1   If you require further advice on the diagnosis and treatment of overtraining syndrome you should contact sportscare UK, 32 Devonshire Street, London W1G 6PX (tel 020-7908 3636).

2   Martin, David E & Coe, Peter N (1992) *Training Distance Runners: the art and science of optimal training.* Champaign, IL, Leisure Press, p264 (out of print).

4.3 Recap and What Next?

Adaptation to training raises the performer's capacity for work. Both physical and psychological adaptation are governed by similar principles.

A balance between training and recovery must be maintained continuously throughout a training programme. The effects of training will not be seen immediately and the emphasis should always be placed on *long-term* improvement.

For further information on some of the topics covered in this chapter, the following books will prove useful. All these resources are available from **Coachwise 1st4sport** (0113-201 5555).

Coaching Focus No 28 (1995) **Focus on: Overtraining and fatigue.** ISSN 02674416.

Dick, FW (1997) **Sports training principles.** 2nd edition. London, A & C Black. ISBN 0 71364 149 5.

National Coaching Foundation (1997) **Physiology and performance.** 3rd edition. Leeds, National Coaching Foundation. ISBN 0 947850 24 4.

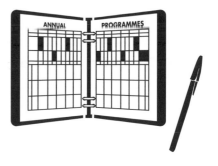

CHAPTER FIVE
Periodization

5.0 What's in It for You?

In Chapter Three, you decided which components of performance to prioritise in your training programme and you set goals with your performer for those components. In Chapter Four, you learned how to plan training programmes for each individual component of performance so that you could achieve these goals. As you must know, however, there is more to a training programme than the sum of its parts. One of the coach's most difficult planning tasks is to fit all the individual components into a yearly training programme. To attempt to develop all components simultaneously would be foolhardy. Time and energy would not allow it and in any case, the training required for some components of performance would interfere with that required for others.

This chapter will help you to divide your performer's/team's programme into separate training periods, each of which will have different goals and training methods. These periods are designed to maximise gains in the different components of performance. The process is called **periodization.**

There are large differences between sports; periodization is therefore highly sport specific. What works for one performer or team may not work for another even in the same sport, so to some extent it is also individual specific. There is no formula that you can take away and apply to all your performers. You must work through the principles of periodization and apply them to your sport and to each performer and team in your care.

The principles which govern periodization are common to all sports, though in some cases the terminology may be used in slightly different ways. In the following chapter you will work through the principles of periodization. This requires you to start at the simplest situation and build your understanding on that. For this reason, the initial activities may or may not be immediately relevant to you. They are a necessary stepping stone to the later sections, so please ensure you understand each section before moving on.

By the end of this chapter, you should be able to:

- explain how periodization can make training programmes more efficient
- divide your season into appropriate training periods
- outline the training content of these periods
- structure your programmes towards achieving longer term goals.

5.1 Training Periodization

There are three layers of training periods that build to form a training programme:

Macro cycles

Meso cycles

Micro cycles.

A **macro cycle** is a period of considerable length aimed at achieving peak performance and can usually culminate in a major competition. Depending on the sport, this period can be anything from a few months to several months. In team sports the macro cycles usually correspond to the annual season, though cycles can be planned over longer periods for world cups and other major competitions, eg Olympic and Commonwealth Games. A macro cycle is divided into several smaller developmental periods called meso cycles.

Meso cycles are subdivisions of macro cycles, usually with a duration of between two and six weeks. Each meso cycle has a specific objective, linked to objectives of the meso cycle preceding and following it.

Micro cycles are training periods of between two and ten days in duration. They contain detailed information regarding the intensity, volume and sequence of training sessions.

5.2 Planning Macro Cycles

A macro cycle is a period of training in which a team or performer aims to produce a training effect leading to peak performance. The length and intensity of the peak will vary according to the sport and the stage of development of the performer/team. In order to produce a peak performance, the macro cycle must be carefully structured, and contain three basic elements:

- preparation period
- competitive period
- recovery period.

The aims of these periods are as follows:

Preparation period: to prepare fully for the demands of competition. Most of the gains in the physical, technical and mental areas will be made in this period.

Competitive period: to maintain the gains of the preparation period and to peak all aspects of performance for major competitions.

Recovery period: to recuperate from the demands of the competitive period, mentally and physically.

This pattern of preparation, competition and recovery is a recurring one. All training cycles must ensure that a period of exertion is followed by one of recovery.

The training programmes of all performers will vary considerably from one period to the next in content and focus. Your first task is to divide your programme into the appropriate periods for your sport. This chapter will help you to make sure you do this in the most effective way.

The division of the programme into these periods is dependent on two important factors:

- The competitive structure of the sport.
- The priorities of the performer.

For many performers and many sports, it is appropriate to use a competitive year as the macro cycle, and divide it into the three periods outlined above. This assumes that there is at least one period in the year when the performers or team will want to compete at their optimal performance level. Some sports will require optimal performance at longer intervals such as two or even four years. In these cases the preparation period may last for two years or more. In this pack at least one competitive peak in a year is assumed, though the same principles will apply to a two-yearly or four-yearly cycle.

In many sports such as football and tennis, performers will compete every week for thirty weeks or more. In such circumstances, it is not possible to maintain a peak of performance for a full season of competition. In these sports, performers will aim to reach a plateau of performance that will be slightly below peak performance, and to maintain this plateau for as long as possible. The principles that will produce that plateau are the same as those that produce a peak.

Even in football or tennis, players will sometimes aim to reach a higher peak of performance for very important competitions. The preparation and recovery periods associated with peaking may make it difficult to play consistently in competitions before and after the peak. Many coaches will prioritise competitions during a season. This allows them to use the less important competitions as preparation for the peak.

Try the next activity. It may be useful to bear a particular performer or team in mind as you complete it.

ACTIVITY 15

1 Study the example below which shows the preparation period, the competition period and the recovery period for a county netball player in the UK.

Jan	Feb	Mar	Apr	May	Jun	Jul	Aug	Sept	Oct	Nov	Dec
Comp				Rec		Prep			Comp		
1	2	3	4	5	6	7	8	9	10	11	12

Figure 9: Seasonal periodization for netball

2 On the sample planner below, mark in the competitive period, preparation period and recovery period for your sport in the first free row:

Jan	Feb	Mar	Apr	May	Jun	Jul	Aug	Sept	Oct	Nov	Dec
1	2	3	4	5	6	7	8	9	10	11	12

3 Consider your own squad or a particular individual. In the second free row, mark in the *major* competitive events, using an asterisk. This will help you to be more detailed in your planning at a later stage.

This may have been quite straightforward or you may have found it difficult, depending on your previous knowledge and your sport. If your sport is one which requires a continuous level of performance over a season, such as netball or rugby, your competitive period will have been quite lengthy. If, on the other hand, your competitive season is very focused on one competition, with other competitions merely used to build to that climax, the competitive period may have been quite short.

The different periods of training are now quite well established for most sports. If your sport requires a number of different competitive peaks in one season you may have found the exercise more difficult, though the same basic principles apply. The next section will help you to apply these principles to more detailed plans.

Double periodization

In Activity 15, an example of a typical single periodized year was shown. For a netball team, this is quite appropriate, as the competitive period is quite long and there is no break of significance during this period. In other sports however, such as swimming, the sport may require the performer to peak for two major competitive periods per year. In this case, your planning will need to have a double periodization. Figure 10 shows an example of a yearly training cycle for a double periodized year.

Sept	Oct	Nov	Dec	Jan	Feb	Mar	Apr	May	Jun	Jul	Aug
Preparation		Competition		R	Preparation			Competition			R
1	2	3	4	5	6	7	8	9	10	11	12

Figure 10: An example of a double periodized year in distance swimming

Some advanced performers may plan for more than two peak periods in a year. This is referred to as multi-periodization. It should only be attempted by those performers who have trained at a high level for several years. Regardless of the number of peaks in a season, each peak must be preceded by a period of preparation, and followed by a period of recovery and transition.

The Preparation Period

In some sports the preparation period is called the pre-season period. It is usually sub-divided into two, a general period and a specific period.

General preparatory period (GPP)

In the general period the emphasis is normally on general conditioning and is characterised by a large quantity of training at low intensities – high volume, low intensity work.

The focus is usually on physical training but it is also a good time for working on technique and applying mental skills to different situations. Practical experience in many sports has shown that performance in the competitive period is substantially determined by the training achieved in the first stage of the preparatory period. If the training load is increased too much in the general period, an inability to sustain performance and peak during the competitive period may result.

The content of the general period would normally include the following:

- **Aerobic fitness training** which provides the foundation of the training pyramid and is the springboard for more intensive activity. Typical activities might include long continuous runs, fartlek training (mixed-pace runs), easy-paced interval training and circuit work.

- **Strength training** to develop a solid base from which to work. This will concentrate on improving strength in the major muscle groups and those specifically required for your sport. It is a time for eliminating individual deficiencies and strengthening weaknesses (eg speed, explosive leg power, upper body strength).

- **Muscular endurance training** (if this is a key quality in your sport). Training in the preparation period should include a variety of speed and endurance training sessions.

- Time for working on individual **technical skills** within your sport. This may include the improvement and/or maintenance of existing technique and the learning of new skills. It may be possible to combine technical sessions with fitness sessions.

- **Mental skills training** should be a key component of this period. This is the time for establishing the base skills in areas such as concentration and relaxation. The skills need to be developed in this period before they can be applied in competition.

Specific preparatory period (SPP)

The specific period is characterised by an increased intensity and specialisation of training – the training becomes more competition specific. The specific period is a transition between the general preparatory period and the early competition period. Skills are honed to a fine edge, so they can be performed under the pressures of competition. Simulated competition exercises may be used to prepare performers for the competitive situation. The content of the specific period would normally include the following:

- **Technical/tactical work** should focus on individual skills and unit, team and tactical training if appropriate. For example, a rugby team may decide to concentrate on scrummaging in this period and could combine tactics and technique with power training.

- **Physical training** should be sport-specific (eg marathon runners should concentrate on being able to repeat distances at race pace). High intensity training should be planned to build up to the important competitive period. This is complicated in some sports (eg team games), in which performers are expected to perform to high levels over a period of several weeks or even months. Weekly training must be designed to prepare performers to peak regularly on game days. In other sports (eg track and field athletics or swimming), performers typically train to peak for major competitions. The build-up is therefore more gradual and early season competitions are used for training purposes.

- **Mental skills training** can now begin to become more specific and should be integrated into each training session. This period provides the opportunity to put into practice some of the mental skills developed in the general preparatory periods. You may begin to encourage performers to monitor their own feelings and moods. Specific pre-competition routines need to be established; coping strategies must be decided on for dealing with unexpected events.

The SPP will be shorter than the GPP. As little as two or three weeks may be required to make the transition from training to competition intensity. The length of time this period takes will depend on the individual, and on his or her stage of development. Mature performers will be able to increase the intensity of their training smoothly, and will react rapidly to the change. Those at an earlier stage of development will require more time; trial and error is the best method for determining optimal periodization.

ACTIVITY 16

Using the following table, divide your preparatory period into both general and specific preparatory periods. Remember that you will only have one general preparatory period, but may have more than one specific preparatory period, depending on the structure of your sport.

1	2	3	4	5	6	7	8	9	10	11	12

The Competition Period

The major objective during this period is to compete consistently. Training intensity will rise but training volume should decrease. The overall training load is reduced. Training must take account of the very specific demands and stresses of the forthcoming competition(s). This might mean using a prepared warm-up routine (physical and mental), a specific dietary pattern, planned periods of rest and relaxation between rounds, heats or matches or training at the specific time of a future competition.

Mental and tactical preparation will take the place of physical and technical. The emphasis in the training will move from working on weaknesses to reinforcing the performer's/team's strengths. This helps to ensure that the performer's mind is right for competition.

In team games, and others where performers must perform at a high level once or twice a week for extended periods, the coach has a delicate balance to maintain. Fitness levels will decline unless sufficient maintenance work is scheduled. On the other hand, an attempt to maintain fitness levels through high volume training can lead to fatigue, which will affect performance in competition, and may ultimately develop into an overtraining situation. Careful manipulation of meso cycles and rating of competitions according to opposition quality may allow for training and recovery cycles to be built into seasonal schedules, even without a break in competition. Any breaks in the fixture list must be used wisely.

High volumes of training might be included in a maintenance meso cycle in mid season. Large squads are a luxury that may allow the coach to rest players mid-season, as it becomes necessary and so allow performers to maintain a high fitness level by playing less competitive fixtures.

Tapering

The stresses imposed in training lead to adaptation, but also cause fatigue. This fatigue can prevent a performer from achieving a peak performance. Many coaches are reluctant to reduce training volumes in the lead-in to competition because they fear that training effects will be reversed. It has been demonstrated, however, that training effects reverse more slowly than was once thought. Training induced fatigue will disappear much more quickly than training effects. The coach's task is to manage training so that peak performance can occur in a window between the removal of fatigue and the reversal of training effects.

To prepare your performers for important games or the major goals of the season, you will need to **taper** their training so they will peak for competition. As discussed earlier, duration and frequency equate to total training volume. In the taper period you will manipulate these variables to decrease total training volume in preparation for peak performance.

Tapering also means an increase in simulated training (training which replicates competition conditions) and mental skills practice. Ideally, the training in the taper period will involve sessions that are at an intensity specific to that of a forthcoming competition. When a taper period follows a period of high training volume it is not uncommon for the performer to feel uncoordinated and inefficient. In the first one third of the taper the body needs time to adjust to the unloading programme.

The duration of the taper period varies from performer to performer and from sport to sport. The length of time for unloading training volume varies from 5–28 days or more but in general terms a normal taper is between 10–21 days. The time required to reach performance readiness will depend on factors such as:

- duration of the preparation period
- training volume of the previous months
- requirements of the sport
- duration of the peak period
- individual differences.

Some performers will have the ability to peak very quickly on very few days of low volume (5–7 days). On the other hand, some will take longer (14–28 days) and it is not uncommon to see superior performances in sport during competitions which follow the major competition period. This may be due to less psychological stress or to greater physiological readiness.

The key to physiological and psychological readiness in the competition period is the knowledge that all the preparatory work has been done. This will give the performer(s)/team a confidence in their ability to achieve their goals, and a determination to succeed that no last minute preparations can achieve.

Transition/Recovery Period

There will be at least one period during the programme where the performer will take a break from training. This period is usually short and is concerned with the physical and mental recovery of the performer. It should last for at least three weeks. Preference should be given to general exercises (active recovery), where performers engage in other sports or recreational activities of interest incorporating fun and variety.

If too few demands are placed on the performer during the competitive period, a transitional period may be unnecessary and the performer may move straight into the next preparatory period. However, there should usually be a brief transitional period, perhaps of two to three days, after each important competitive period, before moving on. Often athletes do not feel they have time for this short break, but it is important following a long competitive period.

ACTIVITY 17

1   Using the chart below, mark in the most important competitions in the year for your performer:

Month												
Competition												
Period												
Components												

2   Now include the training periods you identified in the previous exercise:

- Transition
- Preparation – general period
        – specific period
- Competition

3   In Activity 4 you were asked to list the important components of performance in your sport. Insert these qualities into the chart according to the periods when they will be most prominent.

You should now have an idea of how the principles of periodization apply to your sport. How you periodize your year will depend on many factors, including the:

- *competitive structure of the sport*
- *competitions that you prioritise with your performers*
- *stage of development of your performers*
- *number of different components of performance and the priority you place on each.*

Different coaches will divide the training year in different ways. For example, a team games coach who believed that aerobic fitness was the key to success in that sport would have a much longer general preparatory period at the expense of the specific preparatory period. A coach who believed that tactics and teamwork were paramount would do the opposite.

5.3 Meso Cycle Planning

Meso cycles are periods of between two and six weeks which allow you to structure training in greater detail. Each meso cycle will prioritise different components of training. Therefore, meso cycles differ from each other in tasks, structure of contents, forms of training and training load.

A macro cycle could contain between three and twenty meso cycles; the breakdown will depend on how you wish to categorise and group training components. The demands of the sport, the stage of development and degree of specialisation of the performer as well as the length and type of macro cycle will all have an influence. In essence, it is a case of allocating specific time to the different training objectives so the performer can concentrate on developing particular components without interference from other components. There is no right way and experimentation with the periods is often the only way to determine the best breakdown for an individual.

Examples of Meso Cycle Construction

In a rugby player's preparation period, successive meso cycles might increase the intensity of the player's weight training. The aim is to move from the basic strength training of the general preparatory period, to more specific power based exercises as the competitive season approaches. However, if the player wished to make large aerobic gains, he or she would concentrate on endurance prior to the weights programme, rather than attempting simultaneous gains. As the competitive season approaches, more energy is devoted to technical components. Typical meso cycle structure in the preparatory period might be:

Meso cycle name	Number	Content	Duration
General prep 1	1	Introduction	1 week
2	2	Aerobic base work/ intro to strength	3 weeks
3	3	Strength base work	5 weeks
Specific prep 1	4	Power and anaerobic work	3 weeks
2	5	Anaerobic and technical	3 weeks

Training programmes for beginners will focus on basic techniques and fitness components and will require fewer variations in content and methods than programmes for more advanced performers. Advanced programmes will further subdivide the specific preparatory period and the pre-competitive period to achieve more specific outcomes. Mature performers will therefore have more complex programmes, with a greater number of meso cycles. The number of meso cycles in a season can vary from five, for a single-periodized year in a sport with few technical variations, to 25 or more for an advanced performer in a sport with many technical variations. The next activity will give you the opportunity to apply these principles.

ACTIVITY 18

Refer to the planner you compiled in Activity 16. This is the basic structure of your programme.

1 Identify the major competitions of the year and mark them with an asterisk on the following planner:

Month												
	1	2	3	4	5	6	7	8	9	10	11	12
Competition Planner												
Major Training Periods												
Components												
Meso Cycle Planner												

2 Now fill in the major training periods that you identified in the previous activity (ie general and specific preparatory, competition and transition).

3 Try to identify more specifically the stages at which you will focus on the important training components – for example, the movement from general to competition specific techniques and skills. Write these components into the planner in the space provided. This will assist you in your sub-division of the training programme into appropriate meso-cycles.

4 Determine the optimal number of meso cycles for your performer/team for the coming season.

Bear in mind the stage of development of your performer. Remember that peaking will require very high intensity training and should not be attempted by novices more than once in the annual programme.

Remember that there is no correct answer. The priority you place on the different components will determine how you have allocated your time. If you had difficulty allocating specific sections of time to different training components, remember that you will not ignore a component simply because it is not prioritised for a particular meso cycle. The cycles you have associated with specific components are the times when you will allocate extra time to developing these components.

Look back on your plan and ask yourself how it reflects the priority you place on different training components. Would you make any amendments as a result of this reflection?

Manipulating Volume and Intensity

Structuring meso cycles requires manipulation of the volume and intensity of training for different performance components to achieve the required effects in the chosen components. The trade-off between volume and intensity in each component will determine whether gains are made in that component or whether the component is maintained at the required level.

A meso cycle will have a general level of intensity and volume, to which most of the training in that cycle will be pitched. This will reflect the intensity of the components that are dominant in that period. In the competitive period, for example, the majority of the work will be at competition intensity and will focus on competition specific training.

An example of the volume and intensity of a series of meso cycles is shown in Figure 11:

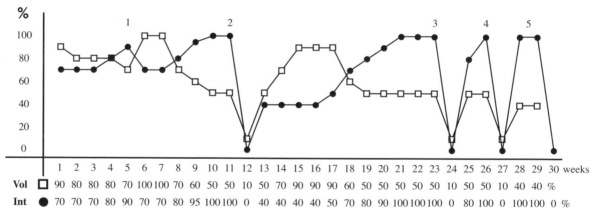

		1	2	3	4	5	6	7	8	9	10	11	12	13	14	15	16	17	18	19	20	21	22	23	24	25	26	27	28	29	30	weeks
Vol	□	90	80	80	80	70	100	100	70	60	50	50	10	50	70	90	90	90	60	50	50	50	50	50	10	50	50	10	40	40		%
Int	●	70	70	70	80	90	70	70	80	95	100	100	0	40	40	40	40	50	70	80	90	100	100	100	0	80	100	0	100	100	0	%

Figure 11: Periods of training within a multiple periodized annual plan for a 30 week competitive season. This plan has one minor peak (1) and four major ones (2/3/4/5)

The next activity will take you through the process of planning your meso cycles. If you are unsure about any stage, go back and read that section of the pack again. This activity will draw on your knowledge of your sport, training principles, planning principles and goal-setting.

ACTIVITY 19

Meso cycle planning:

1 Select a meso cycle from your performer's programme (see Activity 16).

2 Calculate the number of days in the meso cycle.

3 Specify the intensity level of the meso cycle (high, medium, low). This will depend on the distance from competition.

Macro cycle: ....

Meso cycle number: .... Number of days: ....

Intensity level: ....

4 State the objectives of the meso cycle. These may be process or outcome objectives and should conform to SMARTER principles.

Macro cycle objectives:

-
-
-
-
-
-
-

Continued...

5   Identify the components of performance to be developed in this meso cycle and those which should be maintained. State their classifications if appropriate (eg general, special, competition specific). State the percentage of time that should be devoted to each component (an approximate guide).

Component	Classification	% of time	No of units

6   Identify the number of training units for each component in the meso cycle. A training unit is one training session in which you aim to develop or maintain that component. You will decide this based on the principles of training, and whether the component is to be maintained or developed in this cycle. In many cases there will be a trade-off between the different components on the basis of the time available.

7   Identify the length of the micro cycles (eg 7 days) in the meso cycle. This is a matter for judgement. You will need to consider the work/rest ratio for the general meso cycle programme and for each individual component in the meso cycle. A balanced decision should then be made on the optimal length of the micro cycles. The most important physical component is likely to bias the decision, as the work/rest ratio in this will be crucial. Divide the first bar of the following table into the appropriate number of micro cycles.

8   Identify the intensity level of each micro cycle on a scale of 1 to 5 (where 5 is 100% intensity). Then decide the percentage volume. Mark in both levels on the chart provided. An example is provided overleaf.

Length of Micro cycles: .... days

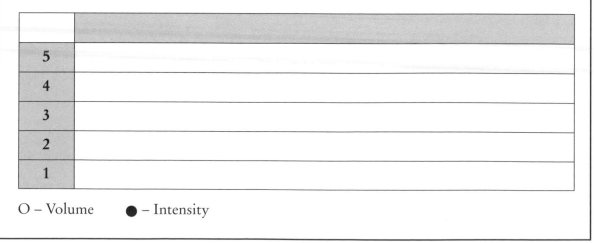

O – Volume   ● – Intensity

Meso cycle plan

Length of Micro cycles: 7 days

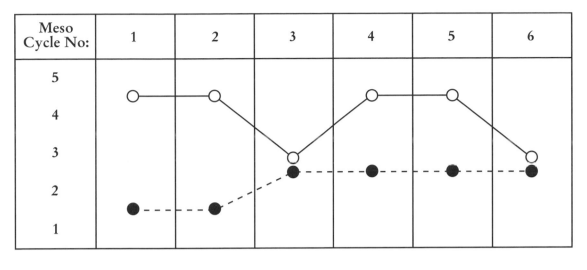

Meso Cycle No:	1	2	3	4	5	6

—O— – Volume   ---●--- – Intensity

Figure 12: Volume and intensity levels in a GPP meso cycle

The way you have planned your micro cycles will depend on the demands of your sport. The number of components and the intensity level will vary. Figure 12 is an example of a general preparatory period meso cycle for a field games player. The intensity level is low but building, and the volume is high, but medium load cycles (3,6) are included to allow for adequate recovery.

The following is a typical meso cycle planner for the competitive period of a volleyball player. It is apparent how the volume and intensity are manipulated according to the principles of overcompensation.

Study this planner. The coach is using a five day micro cycle, with four working days and one rest day. The meso cycle comprises four micro cycles.

A blank meso cycle planner is included in Appendix A.

Macro: Competitive Meso: 11
Objective: Technical – emphasis on blocking/defence. Conditioning – power and speed development; aerobic maintenance

Micro		1					2					3					4				
Date (June)		6	7	8	9	10	11	12	13	14	15	16	17	18	19	20	21	22	23	24	25
Weekday		F	S	S	M	T	W	T	F	S	S	M	T	W	T	F	S	S	M	T	W
Volume		x	x	x	x	x	x	x	x	x	x	x	x	x	x	x	x	x	x	x	x
Intensity (x–Conditioning o–Practice)																					
Day		1	2	3	4	5	1	2	3	4	5	1	2	3	4	5	1	2	3	4	5
C – Conditioning / P – Practice	AM	C	C	P	C	-	C	C	C	P	-	C	C	C	-	-	P	P	C	C	-
	PM	P	P	-	P	-	P	P	P	-	-	P	P	P	P	-	-	-	-	P	P
Practice (1 hr)		3	3	4	3	-	3	3	3	4	-	3	3	3	4	-	4	4	3	3	-
Strength																					
Power		x			x		x		x			x		x					x		
Speed							x							x					x		
Anaerobic																					
Anaerobic A																					
Aerobic			x					x					x							x	
Activity		Blocking	Blocking	Blocking/Defence	Blocking/Defence		Blocking	Defence	Blocking	Blocking/Defence			Defence		Blocking		Blocking/Defence	Blocking/Defence		Blocking/Defence	

Figure 13: Meso cycle planning for a volleyball coach

5.4 Micro Cycle Planning

Micro cycles may be periods of five, eight, ten or any number of days. There is no set time-frame, they should be organised around the objectives of the meso cycle and the principles of adaptation, especially recovery. It is usually convenient to plan micro cycles for a period of one week as this helps to fit training units and sessions into the general framework of social routine.

The smallest training period is the **training unit**, which is a single practice session in pursuit of a training objective. For example, the objective may be to develop concentration skills or sprinting speed. A performer can work on one or several training units in a session. A female basketball player may work through three units in one visit to the gym. She may first work on shooting drills to develop accuracy, then work on a second unit of endurance (eg 12 x 150m sprints with thirty seconds recovery) and in the third unit she may work on her ball receiving skills (eg sealing – moving towards team members to receive the ball early). However, some sessions may be limited by time (eg lunchtime sessions) and perhaps only one unit may be trained. Therefore, training sessions should not be confused with training units, as one session may comprise three units and another only one.

It is useful to rate the intensity of the micro cycle on a scale of one to five, and the volume of training on a similar scale. If the intensity is high and the volume also, adequate recovery must be included. A performer will be able to tolerate consecutive micro cycles of high intensity only if the volume of training is relatively low.

Recovery

Selecting the correct ratio of training units to recovery units is very important in order to facilitate the adaptation process. The demands made on the performer vary from unit to unit. The performer should not be exposed to successive units of very high demand. The intervals between training units should be long enough to allow the performer time to recover and perform in the next unit. Remember recovery is accelerated if it is *active*. When training units of different objectives and varying demands follow each other, complete recovery may not be required (eg a footballer can have a shorter recovery period after a unit of endurance training if the unit following is passing skills). As a rule, more than 24 hours are required to recover from very high loads including competitions.

In most team games, a micro cycle will revolve around a weekly competitive fixture. Most coaches will allow at least a day's rest prior to competition, and will reduce training loads on the previous day or even two. If this mini-taper occurs in every micro cycle, there is little time for intense training in-season. Training time may be further decreased if there are two competitive fixtures in some weeks, and when players carry knocks from game to game and so reduce their training capacity. That is why the fitness levels of many team sport players decline over a season. A coach must plan micro cycles very carefully to minimise this effect. The next activity will help you to sequence your training units in the micro cycle.

ACTIVITY 20

1   Identify the specific goals of the competition period in your sport:

2 Based on the goals you have just set, devise a micro cycle from the competition period for your performer, including all the components of training relevant to this part of the season. Indicate the demand of each training unit on the athlete on a scale of high, medium or low:

Day	Goal	Unit	Demand
Sunday			
Monday			
Tuesday			
Wednesday			
Thursday			
Friday			
Saturday			

Now turn over.

The construction of a micro cycle is based on the principles of sequencing (the correct ordering and spacing of training sessions). Sessions must be sequenced appropriately if the maximum benefit is to be gained. The interplay of loading, resting, training intensity and training volume must be understood if the process is to be managed effectively.

The following list, adapted from Dick, FW (2002) **Sports Training Principles**[1] *gives a comprehensive list of the many factors which must be considered when sequencing training:*

- *Demands in individual training units vary from high to slight.*

- *The performer should not be exposed to very high demands in successive units.*

- *Each training unit should be in pursuit of a specific objective.*

- *Programme planning should include variety and have variations in units that are aimed at the same goal.*

- *Performers require a sense of routine in their programme.*

- *Intervals between two training units should be long enough to allow the performer to recover and work in the next unit.*

- *Recovery is accelerated with active recovery or regeneration units.*

- *When units with different objectives and varying demands follow each other it may not be necessary to wait for complete recovery.*

- *Micro cycles permit concentration on one particular objective in individual units, allowing some optimal period of time when the performer can be exposed to the desired stimulus.*

- *Micro cycles reduce monotony in training despite high frequency of training units.*

- *In terms of physical preparation, demands on speed, power, maximum strength should never follow days of high demand. Speed endurance or strength endurance, should never precede techniques, speed, elastic strength or maximal strength either in the same day or consecutive days.*

In team games, a micro cycle may require a mini taper built in to prepare for competition at the end of the week. Maintenance work on fitness should take place in the early days of the week, so that the training load is lightened prior to competition.

Examine the following micro cycle planner for swimming to see the application of these principles:

---

1   For further information on this, or any other text listed, you should read the *Recap and What Next?* Section at the end of this chapter.

Day		Goal	Unit (see scale below)	Demand
Sunday		Rest		
Monday	am	Aerobic	Low aerobic swim mid aerobic kick	low
	pm	Power Lactic	Lower body weights Threshold swim	high medium
Tuesday		Power	Upper body weights Plyometrics Power swim	high high high
Wednesday		Rest	Sauna Massage	
Thursday	am pm	Aerobic Power Power Aerobic	Low aerobic swim Lower body weights Plyometrics Mid aerobic swim – odds cruise, even build	low high high low
Friday	am pm	Strength Power Power Aerobic	Upper body weights Plyometrics 15m power swims Low aerobic drills mid aerobic pull starts/turns	high high high low medium low
Saturday		Aerobic	Mid aerobic kick Swim lact max swim	medium high

Figure 14: Micro cycle planner for sprint swimmer

Scale

Type of Set	Heart Rate	Lactate levels	Rest
Low aerobic	<130	<2	low rest or continuous
Mid aerobic	130–150	1–3	low rest
Threshold	150–170	3–6	10–30 secs
High lactate	180+	6–12	1:2/1:3 work:rest ratio
Lactate max	max	max	1:5/1:10
Alactic	n/a	1–5	full recovery
Power	max	1–5	full recovery

5.5 The Annual Plan

In this section, you can complete your annual plan. This will provide you with the blueprint for your programme of preparation. Even if you are working to a longer schedule (of two or four years) you will find it useful to plan your yearly programme in this way. You will need all the information you have generated in the previous sections of the pack to complete the plan.

Before you draw up your yearly programme, examine the plan on the following page. Figure 15 shows an annual training and competition plan for a club rugby union team, which plays in a league and two cup competitions. The coach has targeted the league and national cup competitions. The team expect to finish in the top two in the league. The coach has targeted league games 6 and 14 (against their closest rivals) for mini-tapers.

Now apply the same process to your sport. There is a blank planner on Page 78 that you may find useful. Activity 21 will take you through the process and explain the planner.

ACTIVITY 21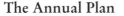

The Annual Plan

Using the blank annual training and competition plan, complete the following tasks:

1 Fill in the months, weekends, all competitive fixtures and their locations.

2 On a separate sheet, rate each competitive fixture on a scale of 1 to 5, five being the most important.

3 On the basis of the fixture rating, insert an asterisk at the weeks where a peak is to be achieved.

4 Identify preparation, competition and transition periods.

5 Break down training cycles into appropriate meso cycles.

6 Fill in the main goals of each meso cycle.

Annual Plan

Month	Weeks (date)	Macro	Meso	Competition	Intensity 1–5	Peaking	Testing
June	6th	General prep	I(a)		2		T
June	13th	General prep	I(a)		2		
June	20th	General prep	I(a)		3		
June	27th	General prep	I(b)		3		
July	4th	General prep	I(b)		3		
July	11th	General prep	I(b)		3		T
July	18th	Spec prep	II(a)		4		
July	25th	Spec prep	II(a)		4		
August	1st	Spec prep	II(a)		4		
August	8th	Spec prep	II(a)		4		
August	15th	Spec prep	II(b)	Challenge (H)	5	★	
August	22nd	Spec prep	II(b)	Challenge (H)	5		
August	29th	Competition	III	Challenge (A)	5		
September	5th	Competition	III	League 1 (H)	5		
September	12th	Competition	III	League 2 (A)	5		
September	19th	Competition	III	League 3 (H)	5		
September	26th	Competition	III	League 4 (A)	3		
October	3rd	Competition	III	Challenge (H)	3		
October	10th	Competition	III	League 5 (H)	4		
October	17th	Competition	III	League 6 (A)	5	★	
October	24th	Competition	III	League 7 (H)	5		
October	31st	Rec	IV	Off	2		
November	7th	Rec	IV	Cup (local)	2		
November	14th	Prep (spec)	V(a)	Cup (local)	3		
November	21st	Prep (spec)	V(a)	Cup (local)	3		
November	28th	Prep (spec)	V(a)	Cup (local)	3		
December	3rd	Prep (spec)	V(a)	Cup/Challenge	3		T
December	12th	Prep (spec)	V(b)	League 8 (A)	4		
December	19th	Prep (spec)	V(b)	Cup/Challenge	4		
December	26th	Competition	VI	Challenge	5	★	
January	2nd	Competition	VI	League 9 (A)	5		
January	9th	Competition	VI	League 10 (H)	5		
January	16th	Competition	VI	Cup/Challenge	5		
January	23rd	Competition	VII	League 11 (H)	3		
January	30th	Competition	VII	League 12 (A)	3		
February	6th	Competition	VII	League 13 (H)	4		
February	13th	Competition	VII	League 14 (A)	5	★	
February	20th	Competition	VIII	League 15 (H)	5		
February	27th	Competition	VIII	League 16 (A)	5		
March	6th	Competition	VIII	Cup RD 1	5		
March	13th	Competition	VIII	Challenge	5		
March	20th	Competition	VIII	Cup RD 2	5		
March	27th	Competition	VIII	Challenge			
April	3rd	Competition	VIII	Cup RD 3			
April	10th	Competition	VIII	Challenge			
April	17th	Recovery	IX				
April	24th	Recovery	IX				
May	1st	Recovery	IX				
May	8th	Recovery	IX				
May	13th	Recovery	IX				
May	22nd	Recovery	IX				
May	29th	Recovery	IX				

Components:
- Base strength / aerobic base / individual (General prep)
- Power speed (Spec prep)
- Tech anaer (August)
- Technical (Competition, Sept–Oct)
- Tech (Rec, November)
- End base (Prep spec, November)
- Ana ero bic (December)
- Technical (Competition, Dec–April)

Goals:
- Individual aerobic/strength goals; Individual strength goals
- Achieve set-piece stability; Develop defensive game plan; Develop offensive game plan
- Develop match patterns: 1 possession, 2 territorial
- Review and develop match Patterns; Review individual fitness levels
- Develop advanced patterns

Figure 15: Annual training and competition plan for a rugby union club side

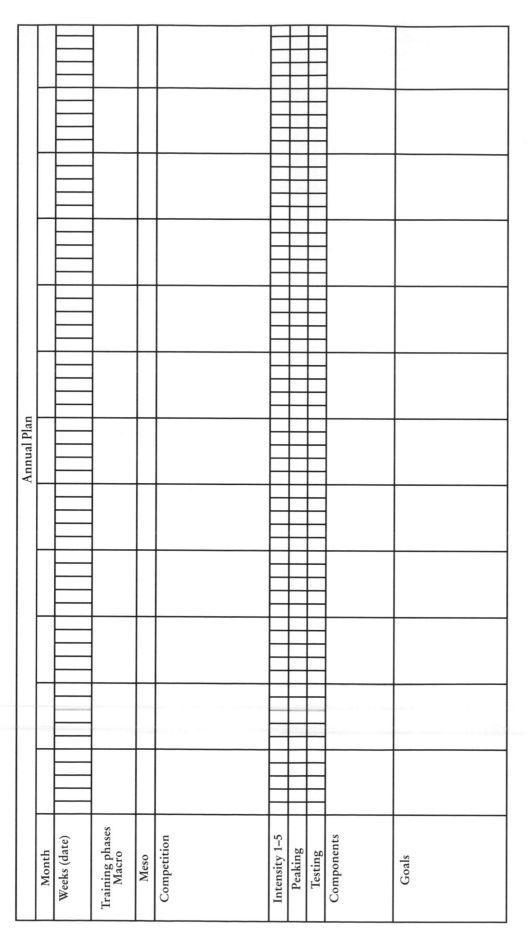

Annual Plan

Month	Weeks (date)	Training phases Macro	Meso	Competition		Intensity 1–5	Peaking	Testing	Components	Goals

If you found this task somewhat difficult, you might like to review the rugby union example and try the activity again.

5.6 Long-term Performer Development Programmes

Training effects are cumulative over years of preparation, and to reach optimal performance takes up to ten years of dedicated preparation. Different experts have classified this long-term preparation into two or three stages. Most agree that in the first two to three years of specialisation in a sport, a performer should focus on a single periodized year. This is often called the *training to train* period. In the next period a double periodized year is possible. Only in the final stage of development should multiple peaks be attempted. There are no strict guidelines for graduation from period to period, although the process of maturation will affect the progression of individuals through the phases.

It is important to remember that a performer may compete at a high level without undertaking a major peaking programme, and all the adjustment of training volume and intensity that peaking entails. The competition period may last for a considerable portion of the year or season, but a performer may attempt to peak for only one particular meet, or one section of the competitive period. These decisions are all part of the planning of the training programme.

Minor peaking schedules may be attempted more often than major peaks. For a minor peak a performer will undertake a mini-taper. This will not have a large effect on their training programmes; the volume and intensity of their training will not deviate too much from the requirements of the meso-cycle. A brief taper (5–6 days) and transition period (1–2 days) can produce mini-peaks, suitable for competitions undertaken in the build-up to major events.

5.7 Recap and What Next?

To improve performance, training units are organised and sequenced into micro cycles for optimal effect. These micro cycles are repeated to form meso cycles and macro cycles. Each period is carefully structured to meet specific objectives.

A balance between training and recovery must be maintained continuously throughout the programme. The effects of training will not be seen immediately and the emphasis should always be placed on *long-term* improvement.

For further information on some of the topics covered in this chapter, the following books may prove useful:

Balyi, I (2002) **Long-term athlete development.** FHS No 14, **sports coach UK**.

Cabral, P and Crisfield, P (1999) **Motivation and mental toughness.** 2nd edition. Leeds, National Coaching Foundation. ISBN 0 902523 24 5.

Dick, F W (2002) **Sports training principles**. 4th edition. London, A & C Black. ISBN 0 713658 65 7.

National Coaching Foundation (1997) **Physiology and performance**. 3rd edition. Leeds, National Coaching Foundation. ISBN 0 947850 24 4.

All these resources are available from **Coachwise 1st4sport** (tel 0113-201 5555 or visit www.1st4sport.com).

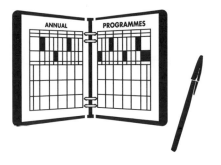

CHAPTER SIX
Time and Lifestyle Management

6.0 What's in It for You?

With so many units of training and recovery to fit into each micro cycle, it is very apparent how sport can dominate a performer's life. You know that many performers are completely focused on their sporting goals, almost to the exclusion of everything else – you also know that such one-dimensional lifestyles are not in the long-term interest of the performer. On the other hand, you will probably have experienced some very talented performers who find it difficult to create time to commit themselves to the training their talent requires, and so never fulfil their potential. How do you strike the right balance between these two extremes?

Your task as coach in this area is twofold:

- You must manage the time your performers spend with you, or in other training tasks, as efficiently and effectively as possible.

- You must help your performers to manage the areas of life over which you have no control, so that their life is full and balanced, without affecting their sporting performance.

These tasks apply equally to coaches of teams and individuals.

This chapter extends your role as coach to that of counsellor, friend and lifestyle manager. These are important skills for a coach, because performance in competition and training cannot be isolated from the rest of a performer's life.

In this chapter, you will examine ways of maximising training time. You will also look at how you might integrate your performers' sporting goals more effectively into their lifestyles. By the end of the chapter, you should be able to:

- make optimal use of the training time available

- help your performers to balance their sport commitments with other lifestyle commitments

- adjust the seasonal plan when unexpected events occur.

6.1 Maximising Training Time

All coaches would like unlimited access to their performers. In the real world, however, very few have such a luxury. Training time is precious and there is rarely enough of it, because each performer will have other commitments to meet outside sport. As coach, you have a responsibility to your performers to ensure the time they commit to training is maximised (used as efficiently as possible).

Each training cycle has objectives that relate to specific components of performance and training time in the cycle is devoted to the pursuit of these. However, the components need not be viewed in isolation. For example, a football player must concentrate on many components of performance (endurance, concentration, anxiety control, passing and so on) during each cycle. If each training session concentrated solely on one component, players would probably never achieve their desired goals. Training sessions will nearly always contain more than one training unit, often they will combine several.

Training units within each training session should be combined where possible, to maximise training time. The footballer's endurance training unit can be combined with a technical, or mental unit, for example. Indeed, it is usually only in the early stages of training a specific component that you will want to train the component in isolation from other components. A football team may have developed concentration skills in the off-season by following very specific mental skills training programmes. As pre-season work commenced, the coach would gradually apply these concentration skills to all training sessions, perhaps beginning with some technical drills and then progressing into practices that simulate competition. The coach could use a training unit of passing skills to work on players' concentration by adding distractions such as other players or background noises. After all, such skills will need to operate simultaneously in competition.

ACTIVITY 22

1   Select a component of performance from your performer's programme, and briefly outline one unit of training for that component, from any stage in the season.

2   Now consider other components of performance that could be integrated into that training unit, without affecting the integrity of the unit.

Now turn over.

You may have decided to combine mental skills with physical or technical, or technical with physical. There are few components that cannot be combined in a training unit.

Training units which require the performer to concentrate on a new component of performance – a new skill or tactic, for example, should not be combined with others. Such units will require the full focus of the performer. In the later stages of honing these skills, additional components may be introduced. Intense physical or mental sessions may not be compatible with complex physical or tactical work, due to the effects of fatigue.

It is important, when attempting to develop components simultaneously, not to create confusion in your performers by asking them to focus on too many goals at once. The following pointers may be useful in preventing a dilution of focus:

• Introduce one aspect of the activity at a time.

• Be very specific in your instructions.

• Seek regular feedback from your performers on their perception of the activity.

Examine the following plans for a training session of a football team and a swimmer. These sessions demonstrate how combinations of activities can achieve several goals in limited training periods.

Date:	23.09	Venue:	25m pool
Main Objectives of Micro cycle:		**Main Objectives of Session:**	
maintain basic endurance levels fine-tune turning/stroke technique improve basic speed 5%		maintenance endurance session stroke technique – holding long basic speed session	
Activity	Unit 1 – 1 hour	**Activity**	Unit 2 – $^1/_2$ hour
W/U: 12 x 75 on 1.15 3 F/C, 3 o/choice, 6 IM order kick 2 x 200 back with 30s rest (1.3km/22) End: 8 x 400 F/C on 5.00 descend for time 1–4–8 (4.5km/57) (Mentally focus on streamlining from turns)		speed/stroke 28 x 25 on 60 No1 stroke technique: max. effort rest 2 minutes at 15 (5.2km/87) (Sprinting but holding stroke long and counting strokes per length)	
Reminders	**Injuries/Other comments**		**Evaluation**
All swimmers to fill in log books this week. Lactate tests next session.	PS low on iron – see dietitian. Video breaststrokers to check injury problems.		Swimmers are adapting well to early prep. work. Should have no difficulties entering next phase.

Figure 16: Sample session plan for a swimmer

The following training session is typical of that of a preparation/pre-season period of a footballer:

Date:	20.10	Venue:	All weather surface
Main Objectives of Micro cycle:		**Main Objectives of Session:**	
maintain aspects of fitness: speed, endurance, flexibility and agility principles of play – possession		endurance maintenance individual positional play to keep possession in attacking third develop concentration on positional play	
Activity	Unit 1 – 60 mins		
1 Warm-up	jogging, stretching, ball touching exercises (10 mins)		
2 Endurance	continuous jogging in positional groups (20 mins)		
3 Recovery	ball work in small groups – maintaining possession (5 mins)		
4 Speed	5 x 50 metres striding, 5 x 50 metres extended stride (10 mins)		
5 Recovery	ball work as above (5 mins)		
6 Education	fluid replacement (10 mins)		
	Unit 2 – 60 mins		
1 Speed	2 x 300 metres (6 x 50 metres) – build up to 9/10 of full speed (10 mins)		
2 Recovery	team play 11v11– maintaining possession attacking 3rd (5 mins)		
3 Tech/Tactics	positional play, set pieces, attacking 3rd (25 mins)		
4 Endurance	continuous jog increasing to striding (15 mins)		
5 Cool-down	stretching and slow jog (5 mins)		
Reminders	**Injuries/Other comments**	**Evaluation**	
Bring running shoes for next training session – long run off road.	TR, AL to see physio next session.	New members of team settling in well. Set pieces and positional play need more work.	

Figure 17: Sample session plan for a football team

The following activity will help you to apply the above information to your own sport.

ACTIVITY 23

1　Refer to Activity 20, Chapter Five and select one training session from the micro cycle you planned.

2　In the following planner, decide on the programme of activities for this session that will maximise the time available and accommodate the different objectives of the session.

Date: ....　Venue: ....　Attendance: ....

Main objectives of micro cycle:

-

-

-

Main objectives of session:

-

-

-

Activity Outline	

Reminders	Injuries/Other comments	Evaluation

Now look over your plan to assess whether the maximum use is made of the time allotted to each activity. It is important that your performers are focused on the activity in hand and know precisely the reason that the activity is being performed and what should be achieved. The trap to avoid is that of trying to do too much in an exercise, practice or session. The NCF home study pack **Planning Coaching Sessions** *(see Section 6.5) will provide more information on this topic.*

6.2 Lifestyle Management

If time is a limited resource, so too is energy. The time and energy available to a performer must be maximised so that training programmes are effective. There are many demands on the time and energy of a performer, both from the requirements of the training programme and from other commitments outside sport (school or work commitments, other sport commitments, family commitments and so on). The effective management of these resources often feels like walking a tightrope. The consequences of a misjudgement can be severe. Lifestyle management is about balancing the demands on a performer's time and energy. It is integral to the coach's task.

Participation in performance-level sport almost always requires a sacrifice in some other area of life (often social or career). This decision can be a difficult one for many performers but well managed lifestyles can help to minimise the disruption. Lifestyle management is an area in which coaches often fear to tread, but the most common cause of dropout from sport, or of failure to reach potential, is a lack of fulfilment in another area of life. This section will help your performers to balance training programmes with the other aspects of their lives.

This section might seem more relevant to coaches in individual sports than team sports. However, team coaches are also coaches of individuals, though they have the added task of blending these individuals into a cohesive team. A team coach must design training programmes to meet the needs of the team, but in developing and implementing it, the coach needs to be sympathetic to the individuals within the team. Every individual will face similar but unique problems balancing home life, work, education and other issues with his or her commitment to sport. Some individuals can find this more difficult than others. In a team sport, morale and team spirit can be adversely affected if the same commitment is not seen to be given by all players. The coach must not avoid these issues. They can contribute significantly, positively and negatively, to performance.

Non-training Stress

Training for sport requires performers to subject themselves to specific stresses, so the body may adapt and become more effective at coping with such stress. Adaptation to any form of stress requires energy, which is a limited resource for every performer. However, there are many sources of stress other than those imposed in training. All these sources of non-training stress also place demands on the finite energy levels of the performer. The more stress imposed by factors external to training, the less energy your performer will have available to cope with the stresses imposed in training.

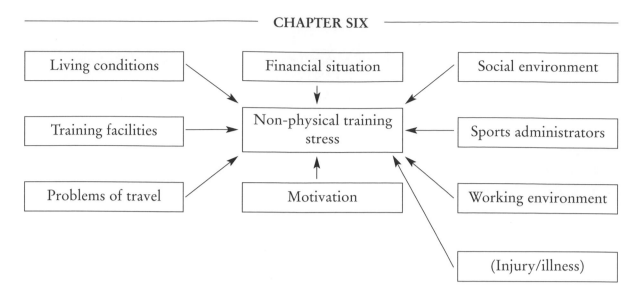

Figure 18: Factors that contribute to non-training stress

Performers will often need help to manage all the conflicting commitments in their lives. This is where your role as friend and counsellor can be most effective. Often performers are so involved in the day to day hustle that they have never stopped to look at the big picture. An objective examination of their lifestyles can provide them with the insight to reassess their priorities and the allocation of their time. You can be the stimulus for this.

Two tools will be of particular help to you in this regard: the **lifestyle audit** and the **lifestyle progress chart**[1]. The former is a snapshot of the current commitments of the performer, and the amount of time devoted to them. The latter is a map of future commitments, in which you endeavour to anticipate and account for future disruptions to the performer's training programme.

Lifestyle audit

To gain maximum benefit from your performers' energy, the use of their time must be planned and rationalised. The lifestyle audit is a tool which will help you and your performers to assess current commitments and priorities. You will then be able to address any disparities in the allocation of time to the different areas of their lives.

ACTIVITY 24

Select a performer from your squad and, in conversation with him or her, complete the following tasks:

1 Select the headings which best describe the important areas in the performer's lifestyle from the following list. Add other headings if necessary:

Work	Education	Family
Social	Sport	Recreation/leisure
Other	....	....

---

1 Coaches face similar time management problems to performers. You may find it useful to use these tools to assess your own lifestyle.

2   In the following table, fill in each box the amount of time (in hours) devoted to each area of life. Use an average week as an example.

	Mon	Tues	Wed	Thurs	Fri	Sat	Sun
Morning							
Afternoon							
Evening							

3   Total the time spent on each area of life, per week:

Work .... hrs

Education .... hrs

Family .... hrs

Social .... hrs

Sport .... hrs

Recreation .... hrs

Other .... hrs

.... hrs

4   Ask your performer to reflect on how this breakdown reflects his or her priorities. Assess how you could reallocate time to reflect them more accurately.

You know that sporting activity is a significant part of your performer's life and indeed of your own. Did you realise how significant? When balanced against the time demands of other commitments external to sport – for example family, study, relationships – the commitment can be seen in a full light.

Lifestyle progress charts

Performers' lifestyles are not static and their priorities are likely to change over time, or as they grow older. It is important to know their current non-training stresses, but you must also know how these are likely to alter in the future. With this knowledge you can be sure that the longer term programmes you plan for and with them are realistic. If the programmes are unrealistic, you will encounter problems with burn-out, lack of motivation and eroding self-confidence. *Lifestyle assessments* can help ensure the long term programmes are realistic.

A lifestyle chart is divided into two parts, one environmental (focusing on family, education and career) and one sport-specific. The example that follows is based on a four year cycle culminating in the Olympic Games, but it could be seasonal or even five yearly. In effect this is a projection of the non-training stresses of the future, allowing the performer and coach to identify significant events in a performer's life, sporting and non-sporting.

Now is the time to start planning for an event that will have a significant effect on your performer's training or commitment to sport, not just before it happens. Events such as examinations, marriages, moving from first to second level or second to third level education, job promotions and so on will have enormous impact on a commitment to sport. Anticipate and deal with them in advance.

ACTIVITY 25

1 Construct a lifestyle progress chart with a performer by completing the boxes in as much detail as possible.

2 You may like to alter the chart and make it more specific to your sport.

	Family	Qualifications Examinations	Career/Progress Ambition	Sporting Goals	Training Structure	Finances
Yr 1						
Yr 2						
Yr 3						
Yr 4						

Now turn over.

Your performers do not operate in a social vacuum. At times, they will have the same significant problems all people face. If you are working with young performers, these difficulties may centre around school, relationships and family. More mature performers will identify different problems and you will need to know about their lifestyle, work demands, demands from home or social demands such as personal relationships.

The lifestyle chart is a tool for monitoring progress and can highlight areas where expert help is required. Practitioners in a range of support services including psychology, nutrition, education and career planning, could be consulted (if required) to give advice.

The two important points to remember with regard to lifestyle management are that:

- well-managed lifestyles are in themselves an enhancement to performance
- everyone involved in sport, including the performer, should ensure that sport does not have a detrimental effect on the life of the individual.

If a performer's lifestyle is incorrectly managed, it can contribute towards a state of increased fatigue and possibly lead to the development of overtraining. Overtraining is covered in more detail in Chapter Five.

6.3 Overcoming Unexpected Events

Regardless of how well you anticipate events, or how well you organise your time and your performer's time, unexpected events will occur which will require you to think again and to reprogramme your preparations. Your performer may become ill or injured, your training facilities may close down unexpectedly due to weather or technical difficulties, your performer may get promoted, fail exams and have to repeat, or undergo any number of personal, work, school or family related events which were unforeseen and disrupt your programme.

In these instances, your ability to adapt and successfully reprogramme the performer's/team's training will be the most significant factor in determining the impact of the event. When an unexpected event occurs, you must **reassess and reprogramme.** This will often mean reduced training loads, or none at all in certain components, until the performer has recovered or the event has passed. The **whole programme** must be altered because of this.

It is tempting to ignore minor inconveniences to your programmes and to carry on regardless. If the event is a minor one, which prevents participation in one component of training only, the performer is likely to be able to carry on with the remainder of the programme, and the effects might appear minimal. For example, a weight room facility might be unavailable for three weeks. However, there is now some excess capacity in the performer's training programme which should be used in order to maximise training time. If it is not taken up by a revised programme, it will be swallowed by another part of the performer's life.

When the performer returns to weight training, it is likely that he or she will need to follow a remedial programme, which will again unbalance the programme. As a result, some other area which should be prioritised during this period will lose out. If the excess capacity was not used in the initial stages, the performer will discover that he or she has lost more ground than was initially obvious. No matter how small the event, the consequences are always likely to be greater than it appears at first.

Facilities Planning

Until something goes wrong, coaches tend to take facilities for granted. When something does go awry, however, inadequate facilities can create havoc with your carefully planned programmes. Things do go wrong – for example, the weather may prevent performers from getting to the training venue or facilities can break down or close unexpectedly. The time for contingency planning and the investigation of alternatives is now – not when it becomes a crisis. The next activity gives you the opportunity to reflect on solutions to potential, rather than actual, problems.

ACTIVITY 26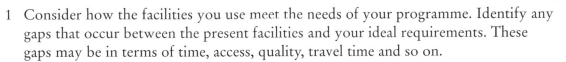

1   Consider how the facilities you use meet the needs of your programme. Identify any gaps that occur between the present facilities and your ideal requirements. These gaps may be in terms of time, access, quality, travel time and so on.

2   Take some time to identify possible solutions to these problems.

3   Now draw up contingency plans in the event of facilities being unavailable due to unforeseen circumstances – weather, breakdowns and so on:

It is very difficult to prepare for unexpected events. However, by carrying out a simple investigation into the facilities you use, it may be possible to limit the damage caused by any unforeseen circumstances.

Rehabilitation of injury/illness

Where a performer has missed a training unit/session or even several days training, it is probably possible to drop back into the programme at the point where he or she would have been without the loss of time. However, where weeks or months have been missed, it is necessary to revise your plans. For example, if you have a performer who has suffered a serious injury and has missed a month's training, there will be a need to reset goals and redevelop your programme to meet the performer's needs.

Because of the principle of reversibility, a performer's level of fitness in all components – physical, technical, tactical and mental – will regress during a period of inactivity. For this reason, any components that may be maintained during a period of injury should be part of an adapted training programme. For example, a knee injury to a rugby player would not preclude mental skills work or upper body strength work, while the knee was recovering.

Remedial programmes

The injured part will require a remedial programme which will be prescribed by the medical practitioner (sports doctor, sports physiotherapist). Always respect medical advice when dealing with remedial exercise, but ensure that the practitioner is experienced in the area of sports injury. In most cases the remedial programme will begin up to one week after the injury. Remedial programmes to injured parts should be continued long after the treatment stops, and even after the return to full competition, to prevent a recurrence of the injury.

Rehabilitative training programmes always require a delicate balance between those components which may be maintained at the level they were at before injury, those which can be developed and the gradual rehabilitation of the components directly affected by the injury. The overall programme must be adapted throughout the period of injury and rehabilitation. Even when full recovery is achieved, the performer's training programme will not simply revert to the pre-injury programme, as some components will have progressed despite the injury, and some will require long-term rehabilitation programmes (as in the case of ankle ligament damage). As progression from cycle to cycle in your initial programme is important, the same principle holds true for rehabilitation from injury or returning from illness. The temptation to accelerate the programme of recovery often leads to chronic problems, as the injury is likely to recur on premature return to competition or full training.

The psychological component of coping with illness or injury is very important. Your performer may experience feelings of low self-confidence and may feel quite helpless. It is essential at this stage to devote a lot of time to maintaining the performer's focus and increasing self-confidence. The coach must be innovative in adjusting the programme and present performers with positive images during any period of layoff – whatever the reason.

6.4 Recap and What Next?

This chapter has highlighted the importance of time management for coach and performer. There is never enough time to do everything, but careful planning can maximise the time available, and ensure that both coach and performer have balanced lifestyles that are conducive to long-term success and enjoyment of their sport.

Often, both coach and performer are so consumed with the present that longer term and contingency planning exercises take a back seat. Attention to both these issues can result in more effective programmes, that can react quickly to adversity, and so increase the chances of overcoming unanticipated events.

For further information on some of the topics covered in this chapter, the following books will prove useful. All the resources listed are available from **Coachwise 1st4sport** (tel 0113-201 5555 or visit www.1st4sport.com).

Cabral, P and Crisfield, P (1999) **Motivation and mental toughness.** 2nd edition. Leeds, National Coaching Foundation. ISBN 0 902523 24 5.

Crisfield, P, Houlston, D and Ledger, P (1996) **Planning coaching sessions: a guide to planning and goal-setting.** Leeds, National Coaching Foundation. ISBN 0 947850 35 X.

Dick, FW (2002) **Sports training principles.** 4th edition. London, A & C Black. ISBN 0 713658 65 7.

sports coach UK (2003) **Sports injury: prevention and first aid management.** Leeds, **sports coach UK, sport**scotland and St Andrews Ambulance Association. ISBN 1 902523 490.

If you require assistance from a sport scientist or sports medicine specialist, the following addresses will be useful:

British Association of Sport and Exercise Sciences (BASES)
Chelsea Close
Off Amberley Road
Armley
Leeds LS12 4HP
Tel: 0113-289 1020

Sportscare UK
32 Devonshire Street
London
W1G 6PX
Tel: 020-7908 3636

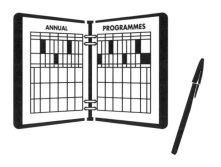

CHAPTER SEVEN
Monitoring Progress

7.0 What's in It for You?

You will now realise that programmes of training progress in small increments. Each training session is a tiny step towards achieving your overall goal. You will want to monitor your progress in this direction, so you know how close you are to where you want to be at any moment in time.

Monitoring is a simple concept and should be a simple process. Many coaches are blinded by science in this area, and often put their performers through comprehensive testing sessions without determining what is strictly necessary. When deciding on how to monitor the progress of your performers, you should use three steps:

- What do you need to know?

- How will you find it out (what measures it)?

- How will you record it and communicate it to your performers?

In Chapter Two, you selected various tests and performance assessment methods which provided you with a snapshot profile of your performers. As you move gradually towards your goals, you will need to know how this snapshot is changing. You will require information on the areas that are improving and any that are not. You will want to monitor the rate of improvement, so you can evaluate the programme of training you have planned and the interventions you have made.

In order to make these judgements, you need some **performance indicators**. Performance indicators are accessible, easily interpreted measurements which allow you to make judgements on your performers' progress towards their goals. You will monitor these indicators so you can adjust the training programme as necessary, in response to your performers' rate of progress.

On completion of this chapter, you should be able to:

- state the performance indicators you will use to monitor your performers

- devise appropriate ways to record your performers' progress

- devise ways to encourage your performers to engage in self-monitoring and record-keeping.

7.1 Performance Indicators

This section examines **why** you might monitor your performers, **how** to monitor them (what indicators to use) and **when** you might monitor these performance indicators.

Why Monitor Progress?

You have already identified several reasons for assessing performers. Coaches test and monitor their performers for many reasons, however, tests/performance assessments can be used to:

- identify strengths and weaknesses of performers to identify priorities
- provide baseline data for individual training programme prescription
- isolate and assess individual components of performance that cannot be measured in the competitive situation
- prescribe the optimal training programme (eg intensity, volume)
- gain feedback to evaluate the existing training programme
- assess the performer's progress – feedback for the performer/coach
- motivate the performer to train
- check the performer has been training correctly (eg putting in the required effort)
- establish homogeneous groupings for training
- assess recovery from injury/lay off.

Your motives for carrying out various tests and assessments will depend on your sport, situation and performers. The next activity requires you to identify some of these reasons.

ACTIVITY 27

Reread the preceding list and make a list of the reasons why you use assessments in your sport:

-

-

-

-

-

-

-

-

-

Now turn over.

You have probably identified many of the reasons listed in the previous section, and some others. Coaches use testing for different reasons – some are very anxious that they have some objective measures upon which to evaluate their training programmes, some use them as motivational tools.

Coaches who have less contact with their performers may use testing more as a monitoring tool than coaches who meet their performers every day. The latter are more likely to be able to make accurate subjective judgements on their performers' current state. Coaches that have infrequent contact with their performers are more likely to use tests to check performers' adherence to training and the efficacy of the training programmes.

How to monitor progress

Your first step is to decide exactly what you need to monitor in order to assess your performers' progress. You may decide it is important for you to have a regular measure of aerobic endurance, for example. It may be that your performer's attitude to training is important to you. You may wish to monitor five areas or twenty-five.

You must then decide on the performance indicators you will use in this process. At this stage you may wish to refer back to Activity 6, Page 21. You may use some of the performance assessments identified on this list as performance indicators. A twelve minute run might provide you with adequate measure of your performer's aerobic endurance; you might use a self rating scale to measure attitude. You may wish to use other measures such as performers' pulse rates or sleep patterns as indicators in other areas. You may wish to monitor some at frequent intervals. Some may be more appropriate to measure infrequently. Whatever you decide, your programme of assessments should provide you with sufficient information about your performers' progress towards their goals.

ACTIVITY 28

1   Decide what areas you need to monitor to assess your performers' progress. List them in the following table:

2   Now list the performance indicator you wish to use in each area:

	area	indicator		area	indicator
1			11		
2			12		
3			13		
4			14		
5			15		
6			16		
7			17		
8			18		
9			19		
10			20		

Make sure you are not over-ambitious in your intentions. Only seek information you need.

Testing performers

Many of these performance indicators will require a programme of testing. The decision on *when* to test is very much a function of the performance indicators you are using, and the reasons why you are testing. When deciding on when to test, bear in mind your periodization of the annual plan. You have divided your training year into segments of time where different components are prioritised. It may be useful to test some components at regular intervals during a training period that has prioritised those components. It is rarely of use to test components in a period where the programme is merely one of maintenance.

Testing too frequently will probably fail to elicit measurable improvements, whereas too long a spell between testing will limit opportunities to evaluate the training programme and to modify it if it is not proving effective. Usually performance improvements will take at least six to eight weeks to materialise, so testing should be structured with this in mind. Most elite performers undergo between two and six tests in a component each year.

Minor competitions can be interpreted as assessments. For example, an international runner may use a county competition as an untapered race to check her current state of training.

ACTIVITY 29

1 Turn to Activity 21, Page 76 and identify when you would test the physical, mental, tactical and technical components of performance. If you want to test all the components within the same micro cycle then simply fill in one square. If, however, you would like to test individual components at varying periods during the season, use a different colour or code to show each component.

2 Would you prefer to administer tests or assessments at:

- specified times during the year
- regular intervals
- one-off testing sessions?

Explain your reasons:

3 Did you involve your performer in deciding on the testing routine?

7.2 Recording the Data

You have identified indicators you will use to monitor your performer's progress. This will produce a lot of data that must be analysed and recorded. You will also want to record other information, such as attendance records and competition results. Coaches can and do record an infinite number of items about their performers and their programmes.

Recording information is time-consuming, however. You must decide what you need and want to record within your programme, otherwise you run the risk of holding lots of useless records, or of failing to record some important data because it was not specific to the task in hand at the time. Most swimming coaches will record swimmers' times in competitive meets, for example, and will usually discuss the swimmers' mental state with them after the event. Some coaches might note some comments on this discussion. This information is relevant only if it is correlated with the records on the results.

ACTIVITY 30

Make a list of the things that in an ideal world, you would **like** to record in your programme:

-

-

-

-

-

-

-

Now turn over.

You will probably have listed many of the following and perhaps some others:

- *The annual periodization chart (including cycles, periods and phases)*
- *Monthly planning sheets*
- *Weekly planning sheets*
- *Session planners*
- *Attendance records*
- *Competition planners*
- *Names, addresses and telephone numbers of performers, coaches, facility staff officials, parents, schools*
- *Progress sheets for all aspects of performance – technical, tactical, physical and mental*
- *Competition result sheets*
- *Goal-setting contract sheets*
- *Testing preparation sheets and testing results (data)*
  - *fitness, mental skills, tactical and technical skills*
  - *biomechanical assessments*
  - *nutritional assessments*
  - *medical screening*
- *Injury report sheets.*

Add any of these to your list if you feel they would be useful. Again, what you record will depend entirely on your situation, sport and performers. For example in a team sport, it is difficult to record everything on every player – you would not have any time left in which to coach. You must develop a system that works best for you – keep it simple but effective. Remember the log is to help you, not constrain or confuse you by holding unnecessary information.

You probably work with a number of performers as individuals or as part of a squad. This makes it difficult to keep regular and accurate records of each one of them, yet such information is vital if progress is to be monitored successfully and objectively. However, it is important you do not create too much work for yourself – use your performers or other members of your coaching team to assist in the recording of information.

The following pages contain various sample sheets which you may find useful for logging information from your programme. More sheets are available in Appendix A for photocopying. Amend any that would be useful with some adaptation.

Performer Personal Details

Name	Address	Telephone (Home/Work)	Date of birth	Education (Work Education/Unemployed)
John Smith	39 Wood Road Leeds LS1 4AP	0113 9949994 (H)	12/10/80	Student, Business Studies, Leeds Met, Year Three. Lives at home

Nutritional Assessment Sheet

Date		Cycle		Period	

Date:
Type of day (eg weekday, holiday)
Level of training load (eg rest day, high intensity)

Time	Training	Detailed description of food/fluid consumed
0600	8k run – h/r 165 28min	Orange juice, wholemeal bread and butter – 2 slices Cereal: Allbran 80g 2 bananas, an apple
0800		

Personal Best Record Sheet

Name	Date	Competition	Event	Result	Position
eg Jill Smith	3.2.97	Grand Prix Swim Meet (Long Course – Leeds)	100m B/fly	1:02.35	3rd Junior
eg Ian Brown Centre	5.7.97	Durham Colts RFU County Plate	2nd Round – Framwell	Scored 2 Tries	Won 18 – 12

Figure 19: Sample monitoring tools (a complete blank version of each of the above and more samples are available to photocopy in Appendix A).

Displaying Progress

Coaches use a diary to log things such as individual session plans or season goals. Items such as attendance sheets and testing data are usually stored on a computer or in a file. All these pieces of information can provide records of progress. For motivational purposes, coaches will usually want to share this information with their performer(s). Notice boards are useful for this purpose.

Many coaches use graphs to display data they want to share with their squads. This gives performers and coach a visual display of progress and can be useful in portraying the overall picture. For example, performance times in training for a specific distance could be graphed over a meso cycle or even season. Figure 20 illustrates how a football coach might illustrate a player's 30 metre sprint speed, tested weekly over a season. The advantage of a graphical display is that trends in the data can be recognised more easily, so the performer does not become too focused on the last result. In week 17 of the graph in **Figure 20**, the result was worse than the previous week. However, the graph reinforces the downward trend, and the poor result for that week should not worry the performer unduly.

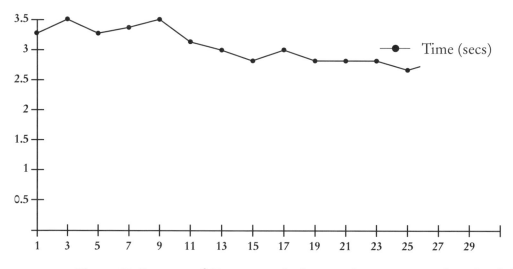

Figure 20: Progress of 30 metre sprinting speed over a season for a footballer

Once you have developed your own organisational and management skills, the people around you will also become more effective at planning and recording information (eg assistant coaches, performers). Throughout this pack, you have been encouraged to include your performers in many planning activities (such as performance profiling and goal-setting) and again it is important that you encourage them to record their own information about their training programmes.

7.3 Performers' Logbooks

Performers from individual sports will often keep a diary or logbook. This practice is not so evident in team games although some coaches do encourage performers to record information about their training and performances. If you discuss your methods of assessment, planning and recording with your performers, it may be possible to combine your requirements with some entries they make in their personal logbook or training diary. This saves you time and will prevent replication.

Your performers can monitor aspects of training, competition and lifestyle such as their own:

- body weight

- resting heart rate

- sleep patterns

- attitude to training

- weekly commitments (eg checking information generated in the lifestyle progress chart)

- pre-competition strategy sheets

- competition evaluation sheets (eg structured debriefing).

ACTIVITY 31

1 If your performers already keep logs, make a list of the things they record and how often (eg every coaching session, once a week, after competition):

Information Recorded	How Often

2 Whether or not they do, make a list of the things you feel would be useful for them to record (eg training goals, competition goals, performance progress, post-competition evaluation) and how frequently (eg every session, competition or weekly):

Information Recorded	How Often

Now turn over.

It may be useful to ask yourself some questions:

Are your suggestions realistic?

Might it become a chore?

Should they always carry their logbook with them?

How frequently do you/should you go through their logbook with them?

You need to decide what would be helpful (and motivating) for your performer. It will also prove invaluable if you could combine some recording of your own with that of your performer – in other words, your performer is entrusted to record his/her own progress.

Sample Self Monitoring Sheets

On Page 109 you will find a sample Self Monitoring Sheet. You may find it a useful framework for your performer's record-keeping or you may wish to customise it in some way.

When using the sheet your performers should:

- plot their resting heart rate, body weight and sleep pattern first thing each morning
- use a different symbol or different coloured pen/pencil for each variable
- plot from left to right but use the appropriate scale for each variable (ie resting heart rate and sleep, read from the left hand axis)
- ensure the days of the month are indicated and synchronised with both graphs
- plot their attitude to training at the end of each day
- keep the monitoring sheet handy (beside the bed?)
- record all four variables consistently over a 3–4 month period to identify normal stress response ranges.

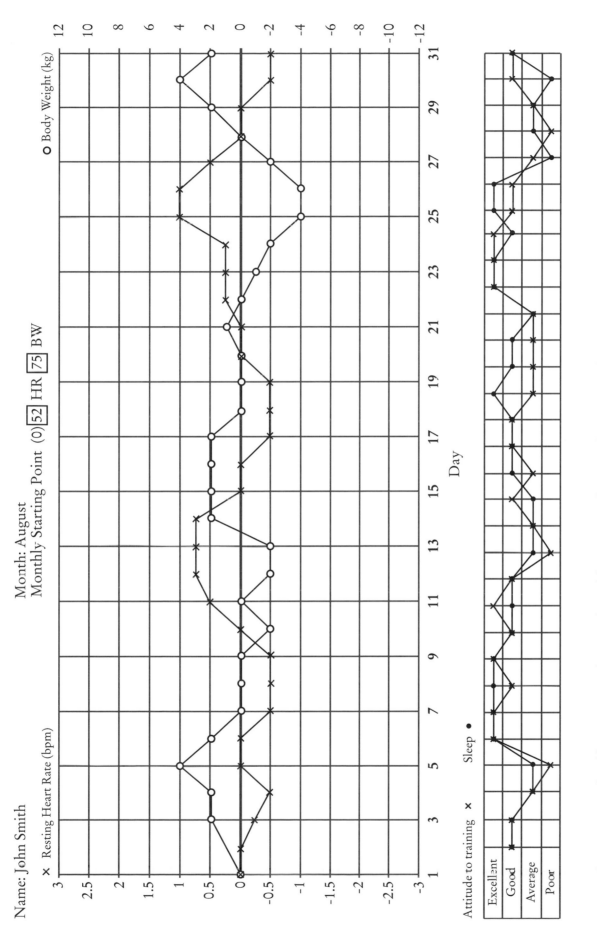

Name: John Smith

Month: August
Monthly Starting Point (O) 52 HR 75 BW

× Resting Heart Rate (bpm)   O Body Weight (kg)

Attitude to training ×   Sleep ●

Excellent	
Good	
Average	
Poor	

Figure 21: Sample self-monitoring sheet (Adapted from: Australian Coaching Council: Recovery Weekly Planner Pack by Angela Calder.)

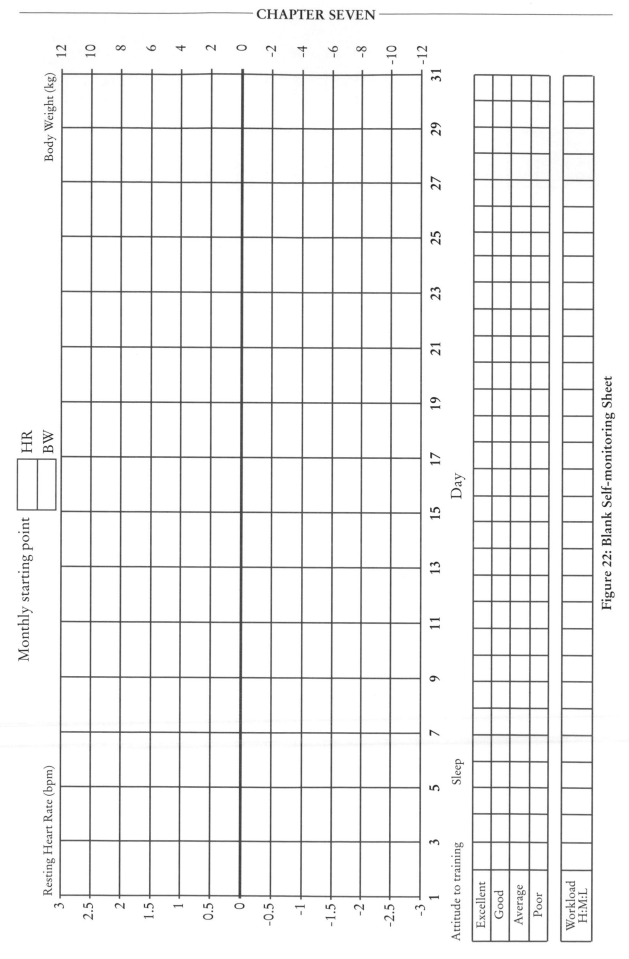

Figure 22: Blank Self-monitoring Sheet

Instructions and important points for using self-monitoring sheets.

The self-monitoring sheet is a useful tool in identifying the signs of overtraining and overuse problems and in the early detection of illness. The monitoring process will encourage your performers to take responsibility and help to *tune them into their bodies and minds.*

Although the responsibility for monitoring certain aspects of performance (eg recovery, training, environment) may be placed on the performer, it is very important that you periodically check your performers' logbooks. Similarly, it is important you emphasise the need for your performers to inform you of any irregularities in their personal records (eg constant tiredness, weight loss, high resting heart rates) as quickly as possible.

Self-assessment forms

Performers can be encouraged to assess their own performance in competition. This process will help them to analyse their performance, to be self-critical and to relate their performance to their personal goals.

Encouraging performers to *look in the mirror* is an effective way of generating commitment to improvement. Many coaches use this process informally. If you wish to formalise the process, review the following example used by a football coach.

ACTIVITY 32

Example of a post match assessment sheet for a football defender:

1 Write down your goal(s) or specific task(s) for the match (eg marking a specific opponent):

2 Did you achieve your goal(s)? Yes/No

If you elected to change your goal(s) prior to the start, explain why:

3 How do you feel about your performance?

Very satisfied   Very disappointed

    5   4   3   2   1

4 Describe the conditions (eg pitch condition, weather, reorganisation due to injury or sending off):

How well did you cope with the conditions?

Very satisfied   Very disappointed

5   4   3   2   1

5 How well did you stick to your pre-match plans:

• prior to arrival at the ground?

Exactly   Not at all

5   4   3   2   1

If less than 4, explain why:

• at the ground?

Exactly   Not at all

5   4   3   2   1

If less than 4, explain why:

Continued...

6 How well did you carry out your warm-up?

Very well   Very badly

5   4   3   2   1

Explain why:

7 How well did you concentrate:

- during the warm-up?

Very well   Very badly

5   4   3   2   1

- during the first early stages of the match?

Very well   Very badly

5   4   3   2   1

- during the middle phase of the match?

Very well   Very badly

5   4   3   2   1

- towards the end of the match?

Very well   Very badly

5   4   3   2   1

8 What percentage of the time did you keep control of your emotions?

100%   80%   60%   40%   20%   10%

Expand if necessary:

9 Write down any other positive thoughts about the competition:

10 Write down any other negative thoughts about the competition:

11 How much did you enjoy the competition?

This is a comprehensive post-event assessment sheet. It may be that the information you require from your performers can be collected in a more concise form. Again, do not collect information for the sake of it. Review your requirements and construct a mechanism for collating the necessary information.

When considering pre- or post-event assessments, remember that a performer will often find it easier to be honest when writing to a form than when talking face-to-face. A form also allows time to think without the pressure of having to generate an immediate response. For these reasons it can be better than an interview.

7.4 Recap and What Next?

This chapter focused on monitoring the progress of your performers and programme. It examined testing procedures and recording strategies. It is important that you become highly familiar with the guidelines for testing and develop your own procedures which are both systematic and effective. In terms of recording information there is no right or wrong answer. It is important to log and record training information in order to monitor progress, but at a level that suits you, your performers and your sport.

The following will complement the information given in this chapter:

Bale, P and Doust, J (1992) **Measuring body fat: a guide to body fat and its measurement using the slimguide calliper.** (Booklet and callipers) Leeds, National Coaching Foundation. ISBN 0 947850 88 0.

Brewer, J, Ramsbottom, R and Williams, C (1998) **Multistage fitness test.** 2nd edition. Leeds, National Coaching Foundation. ISBN 0 902523 06 7.

Calder, A (1994) **Recovery programmes.** Home study pack for the Australian Coaching Council's Graduate Diploma of Sports Coaching.

Davis, J (1996) **Fitness for games players.** Leeds, National Coaching Foundation. ISBN 0 947850 10 4.

Wilkinson, D and Moore, P (1995) **A guide to field based fitness testing.** Leeds, National Coaching Foundation. ISBN 0 947850 55 4.

All these resources are available from **Coachwise 1st4sport** (tel 0113-201 5555 or visit www.1st4sport.com).

To continue to update and develop your coaching knowledge and skills, you are advised to take note of the workshops and resources recommended throughout the book. These will help to extend your knowledge further on specific topics and improve your coaching.

Recommended **scUK** workshops and resources (complimentary with the corresponding workshop) include:

scUK Workshop	Resource
A Guide to Mentoring Sports Coaches	A Guide to Mentoring Sports Coaches
Analysing your Coaching	Analysing your Coaching
Coaching and the Law	–
Coaching Children and Young People	Coaching Young Performers
Coaching Disabled Performers	Coaching Disabled Performers
Coaching Methods and Communication	The Successful Coach
Equity in Your Coaching	Equity in Your Coaching
Field Based Fitness Testing	A Guide to Field Based Fitness Testing
Fitness and Training	Physiology and Performance
Fuelling Performers	Fuelling Performers
Goal-setting and Planning	Planning Coaching Programmes
Good Practice and Child Protection	Protecting Children
Imagery Training	Imagery Training
Improving Practices and Skill	Improving Practices and Skill
Injury Prevention and Management	Sports Injury
Motivation and Mental Toughness	Motivation and Mental Toughness
Observation, Analysis and Video	Observation, Analysis and Video
Performance Profiling	Performance Profiling
The Responsible Sports Coach	–
Understanding Eating Disorders	–

Details of all **scUK** resources are available from:

Coachwise 1st4sport
Chelsea Close
Off Amberley Road
Armley
Leeds
LS12 4HP
Tel: 0113-201 5555
Fax: 0113-231 9606
E-mail: enquiries@1st4sport.com
Website: www.1st4sport.com

The **scUK** also produces a technical journal – *Faster, Higher, Stronger (FHS)* and an information update service for coaches (**sports coach update**). Details of these services are available from:

sports coach UK
114 Cardigan Road
Headingley
Leeds
LS6 3BJ
Tel: 0113-274 4802
Fax: 0113-275 5019
E-mail: coaching@sportscoachuk.org
Website: www.sportscoachuk.org

For general information about **sports coach UK** workshops, contact the Workshop Booking Centre on 0845-601 3054. For details of workshops running in your area, contact your nearest Regional Training Unit (RTU) or home countries office or visit www.sportscoachuk.org. RTU details are available on the **sports coach UK** website.

APPENDIX A
Useful Planning and Monitoring Tools

Amend and photocopy these tools as you require them.

Individual Record Sheets

122 Performer details

123 Performer assessment record

124 Injury report

125 Goal planner

127 Performer profile form

Planning Tools

128 Season planner

129 Meso cycle planner

130 Micro cycle planner

131 Session planner

Assessment Tools

132 Self-monitoring tools

133 Lifestyle audit

134 Lifestyle progress chart

135 Nutritional assessment sheet

136 Opposition analysis (performer)

137 Opposition analysis (team)

Performer details			
Name		Home phone	
Address			
Work/school		Phone	
Next-of-kin		Phone	
Date of birth			

Club		Position/Event	
History			

Personal best performances/Representative honours			
Date	Venue	Details	Comment

Medical details			
Date	Condition	Medication	Comment

Performer Assessment Record	
Performer name	

Physical							
Test	Dates						

Technical							
Test	Dates						

Mental							
Test	Dates						

Injury Report			
Date		Event	
Name of injured person			
Details of injury			
Where it happened			
What happened			
Time			
Witness(es)			
Action taken			
Treatment/action /referral			
(if appropriate) Name of medical personnel involved			
Hospital/centre attended			
Guardian informed			
Post injury notes			
Signature of coach			

Goal Planner (Fill one for each long-term goal														
		Achieved by												
		Weekly goals												
Long-term Goal:	Monthly goal													

Goal Planner (Fill one for each long-term goal)

Performer Profile Form

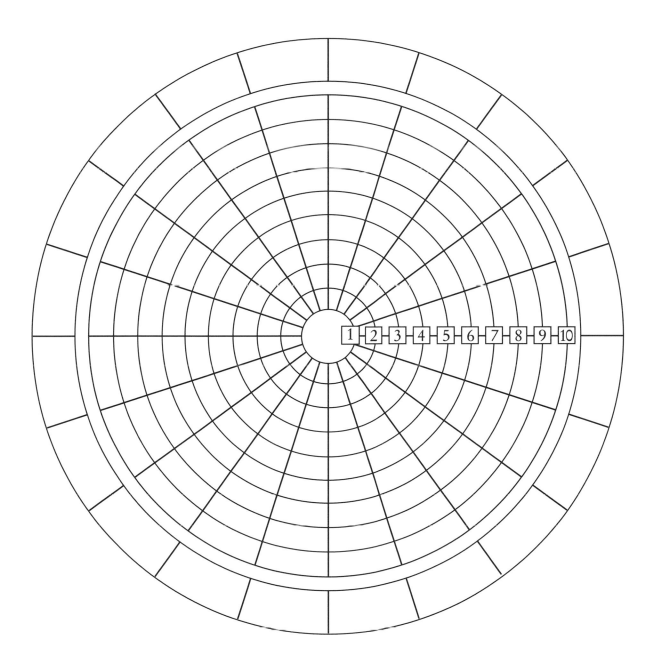

Season Planner

Annual Plan

Month	Weeks (date)	Training phases Macro	Meso	Competition		Intensity 1-5	Peaking	Testing	Components	Goals

Meso cycle Planner

Macro cycle:
Objective:

Meso cycle:

Date	Weekday	Volume	Intensity	Day	AM	PM								Activity
		5	5											
		4	4											
		3	3											
		2	2											
		1	1											
		0	0											

Micro cycle Planner			
Day	Goal	Unit	Demand
Sunday			
Monday			
Tuesday			
Wednesday			
Thursday			
Friday			
Saturday			

Session Planner	
Date	
Venue	
Attendance	

Main objectives of micro cycle	**Main objectives of session**

Activity outline		

Reminders	**Injuries/Other comments**	**Evaluation**

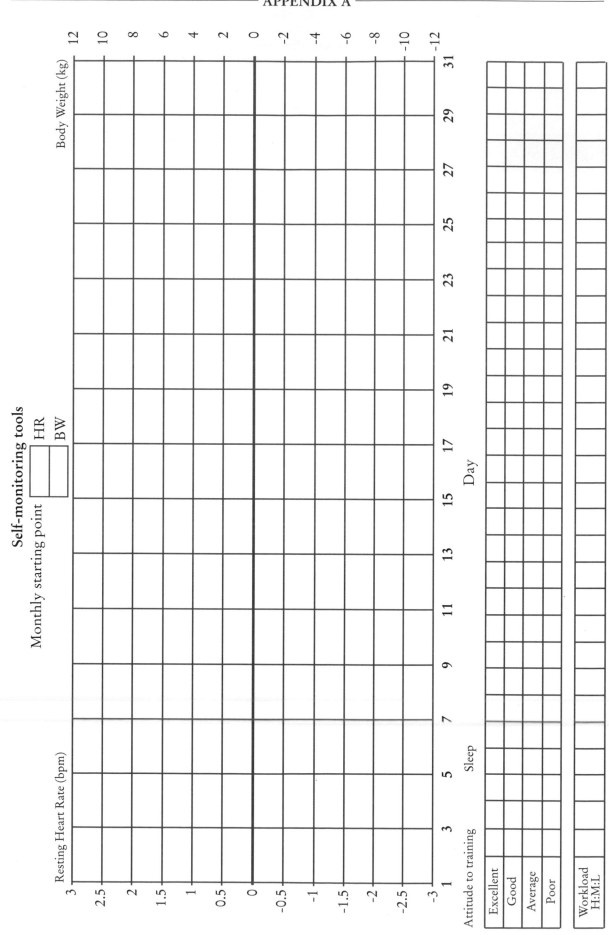

Lifestyle Audit

	Mon	Tues	Wed	Thurs	Fri	Sat	Sun
Morning							
Afternoon							
Evening							

Lifestyle Progress Chart

	Qualifications Examinations	Career/progress Ambition	Sporting Goals	Training Structure	Finances
Family					
Yr 1					
Yr 2					
Yr 3					
Yr 4					

Nutritional Assessment Sheet					
Date		**Cycle**		**Period**	
Date					
Type of day (eg weekday, holiday)					
Level of training load (eg rest day, high intensity)					
Time		**Training**		**Detailed description of food/fluid consumed**	

Opposition analysis (performer)			
Date		Time	
Opposition		Venue	

Player	Strengths	Weaknesses

Other factors

Opposition analysis (team)			
Date		Time	
Opposition		Venue	

Team strengths	Team weaknesses

Other factors